MAKE ROOM TO GROW

Make Room to Grow

*Transform the Church
without
Killing the Congregation*

Jeffrey E. Greenway

ABINGDON PRESS
Nashville

MAKE ROOM TO GROW: TRANSFORM THE CHURCH
WITHOUT KILLING THE CONGREGATION

This book is printed on acid-free paper.

Library of Congress Cataloging-in-Publication Data

Greenway, Jeffrey E., 1960–
  Make room to grow: transform the church without killing the congregation / Jeffrey E.
Greenway.
      p.   cm.
  ISBN 978-0-687-49155-1 (binding: pbk.: alk. paper)
  1. Church growth.   I. Title.

BV652.25.G724   2007
253—dc22
                                                                          2007002041

07 08 09 10 11 12 13 14 15 16—10 9 8 7 6 5 4 3 2 1

MANUFACTURED IN THE UNITED STATES OF AMERICA

... In praise of God who saved me in Christ.
... In dependence upon the Spirit who convicts, converts, and consecrates.
... In gratitude to parents, Harold and Betty Jo, who brought me into the world and taught me the things of God.
... In relationship with Beth who loves me deeply and unconditionally.
... In thanksgiving for our kids, Nathan, Joe, and Paige, who remind me that relationships are what really matter.
... In debt to people who have spoken truth into my life and called me to be more than I am.
... In appreciation for the churches in Butler, PA; Erie, PA; Pittsburgh, PA; Wilmore, KY, and Reynoldsburg, OH that have given me glimpses of what it means to be in the body of Christ.
... In grateful thanks to Sheila Lovell and Kelly Hahn from Asbury Seminary, without whom this work would never have been completed.
... And in utter humility that God calls human beings to proclaim the depth of grace and lead the Church in change and transformation ... may our tribe increase!

CONTENTS

RINGING THE TREE: A METAPHOR FOR CHANGE IN THE POSTMODERN AGE

A few years ago, my wife, Beth, and I were graciously given a weekend stay at a bed-and-breakfast near Titusville, Pennsylvania. Titusville is located in an area where 90 percent of the veneer-quality black cherry timber in the world grows; the wooded lots outside our window were filled with this cash crop. In fact, as we arrived, the owner of the farm was dragging a forty-foot black cherry veneer log he had just finished toppling.

"How much would a tree like that earn for you?" I asked.

"About $40,000," he replied. I acted as if I expected that answer, but inside my mind was yammering, *Forty grand? For a tree! Really!*

Throughout our stay, I became increasingly intrigued by life and work on the hardwood lumber farm. As we toured the family property, I struck up a friendship with the trail guide. He was the owner's son, and he had graduated from West Virginia University with a degree in forestry. He managed the forests of a major paper company during the week, but on weekends he helped with his dad's crop.

During one of our rides through the forest, I received a crash-course lesson in hardwood lumber management. As we came upon a grove of trees, I noticed a massive maple tree looming over several other smaller trees. Its trunk was at least three feet in diameter, and its branches wove their way from the trunk with elegance and grace. It would have been perfect for our back-yard—sturdy enough to hold a tree house or rope swing, yet expansive enough for older adults to recline in its shade. Surrounding the maple were about a dozen smaller hardwood trees: white oak, red oak, black walnut, and black cherry.

The owner's son asked me which tree I thought was the most valuable. Still impressed by its character and presence, I jerked a thumb at the maple tree. He looked at the maple and cocked his head.

"That might look great in a backyard...but to me it's just pretty-lookin' firewood."

The former forestry major then began to teach us that the real value of the forest was located in the dozen or more trees within thirty feet of that majestic maple. They were tall, slender, and straight—veneer logs with the potential to be used in the furniture-building industry. He pointed out trees that were *already* worth $10,000, $20,000, and $30,000. But to ensure the profitability of the family's future, he needed to manage the hard-wood forest now, and it turned out that the stately maple tree I had been so taken with was hoarding nutrients that would help the hardwood trees grow. Worse, if the maple were to topple over, it would cause extensive (and expensive) damage to the more profitable trees. It became apparent to me that the maple tree would have to go.

Our guide then asked what I would do if I were managing this section of the forest.

"Well, given that the maple is sapping nutrients from the other trees, I guess I would crank up the chainsaw and cut her down," I said, chuckling.

"That's too risky," he said, seriously. "What if the tree fell the wrong way and landed on one of the cash crop trees?"

"That would be a very expensive mistake," I said, abandoning any subliminal dreams of a future in forestry. "So what do you do?"

"What we do," he said, walking slowly to the maple and then tracing his finger around its trunk, "is what we call 'ringing the tree.'" Our guide then proceeded to give us a fascinating lesson in forest management that I believe serves as a metaphor for facilitating change in the church as we settle into postmodernity.

Ringing a tree involves cutting two circles deep into the tree's base—about one foot apart from each other. Doing so cuts off the flow of nutrients at the ground level, effectively redirecting them through the various root systems to the other trees in the grove. Unable to receive the necessary nutrients, the unwanted tree begins to die slowly. First, the branches near the top of the tree decay from the outside in. Next, the starvation process continues in a top-down fashion—all the way down to the trunk. Finally, the tree dies, *yet does so in a way that causes no harm to the other trees.* Not only would the maple no longer receive the ground's nutrients; the walnut, black cherry, and other, more harvestable trees would mature more quickly.

As we rode from grove to grove, I saw dozens of trees that had been ringed and were in various stages of dying from the outside in. The contrast was startling; vital, healthy, gorgeous trees were towering over their shriveled, emaciated, and dying counter-parts—signs of a profitable future.

I think the technique of "ringing the tree" is an apt metaphor for anyone preparing for—or already engaged in—local church ministry. All too often, we see outdated systems, methods of communication, or even long standing traditions, and want to fire up the chainsaw, much as I did in that tree-farmer's grove. But what will happen when we take such a drastic measure with that "tree"? We may succeed in creating change, but we will likely also damage nearby healthy, budding trees in the process. Max De Pree wisely notes in his book *Leadership Jazz*, "Followers, not leaders, accomplish the work of the organization. We need to be concerned, therefore, with how the followers deal with change" (Max De Pree, *Leadership Jazz* [New York: Doubleday, 1992], 28). In other words, chainsaws don't just hurt the tree; they hurt everybody.

"Ringing the tree" means introducing change without cutting down or uprooting the old systems, structures, or styles. We simply stop feeding them the nutrients they require to survive and let nature take its course. It also means beginning to feed new systems, structures, and styles we believe will foster growth and life in the service of a profitable, God-paved future.

Make Room to Grow: Transform the Church without Killing the Congregation is my account of how one church transitioned from a hierarchical, bureaucratic style of ministry to one carried out by the saints themselves. We made plenty of changes and we didn't get every one of them right. But we were convinced we could not maintain the status quo and be faithful to God's mission.

Most books on change take for granted that leaders will quickly scrap anything (or anyone) *old* or in the way, thus placing most of their emphasis on introducing whatever is *new*. As a former pastor and district superintendent, I will assume you *can't* do that. The truth is that nothing dies quickly in the church. Processes, traditions, ways of thinking, and ideologies lag over years, decades... even centuries. With tongue in cheek, Leonard Sweet and Brian McLaren identify contemporary worship as "...worship that is 30 years behind the times instead of 150 to 300 years" (Leonard Sweet, Brian D. McLaren, and Jerry Haselmayer, *A is for Abductive: The Language of the Emerging Church* [Grand Rapids: Zondervan, 2003], 76). Get used to it: the old and the new often have to live together.

Yet that is no excuse for ignoring areas in the church that desperately need to be changed. My hope is that my story of the transition at Christ United Methodist Church in Erie, Pennsylvania will help you make wise, loving, mission-based changes in an organic way that honors Jesus and unifies the church.

CHAPTER ONE

❧ ⚜ ❧ ⚜ ❧ ⚜ ❧ ⚜ ❧ ⚜ ❧ ⚜ ❧ ⚜ ❧ ⚜ ❧

CHALLENGING SPIRITS, CHANGING STRUCTURES

"People are always as creative as the structure allows them to be."
—Rick Warren, *The Purpose Driven™ Church*

"I once attended a church that had so many committees it even had a 'Committee of Committees' to keep all the other committees organized. That's too many committees."
—Tim Stevens and Tony Morgan, *Simply Strategic Stuff*

Given the postmodern age in which we find ourselves and its implications for ministry, how does the leadership of a congregation shift its ministry style from the top-down, organizational, hierarchical, permission-withholding, pastor-centered, corporate model of the 1950s to a bottom-up, organic, collegial, permission-giving, team-oriented model centered around the spiritual giftedness of its members in the twenty-first century? Does it happen best through the dissemination of responsibilities through various committees? Does it happen by randomly assigning individuals to undertake significant ministry tasks? Does it happen by letting the pastor do all the work while others pat him or her on the back? You might be thinking, "No," but many churches operate from this very paradigm. In the process, budding ministries are squeezed out by the church's infrastructure, or willing servants are slotted into ministry areas where they don't belong. Perhaps the following story will set the stage for the problems we faced at Christ Church.

1

A man and a woman fell deeply in love. They married and moved into a small, one-bedroom apartment. It was quaint and cozy. They ate there. They slept there. They talked there. They played there. The apartment was sufficient for their domestic needs. Their love nest provided them with a place they could call their own. They learned that two don't live as cheaply as one, but they adjusted and were able to make ends meet. They both shared the work of keeping their home livable and presentable within clearly defined roles.

They dreamed of starting a family. After a few months, they got the news—she was pregnant. They sorted through baby names and looked at wallpaper—baseballs for a boy, flowers for a girl. But a few months into the pregnancy, they received news they had not anticipated: they were expecting triplets. One look around their love nest and they knew they would have to move.

Unfortunately, when the babies came the job market was lousy, interest rates were outrageous, and the family could not afford to move out of their small, one-bedroom apartment. The three babies slept in the one bedroom. The mother slept on the sofa. The father slept on the floor (after a painful experiment in the bathtub). Pockets of quiet were impossible to find. The family budget—already strained prior to diapers, formula, baby clothes, etc.—was constantly stretched.

And meals? Whereas the mother and father had once enjoyed intimate dinners with soft music in the background, they now could not even eat together. Sleeping, when possible, was done in shifts. They were living on top of one another, relationally drained from raising a super-sized family in an old space, on an old budget, and with an old understanding of roles. Neither parent wished the children hadn't been given to them, but both, when life was at its most frenzied, would think to themselves in a panicked way: *This is not sustainable. This is NOT sustainable!*

Everything had changed.

I felt a lot like that couple when I pastored Christ United Methodist Church in Erie, Pennsylvania. Before I arrived, it was a midsize church with a small budget and a projected deficit. But during my tenure, we grew to approximately nine hundred members, with an average attendance of three hundred sixty in worship, a church school averaging one hundred ninety-two students, and an $800,000 budget with no projected deficits. You could say our church body went from living (metaphorically) in a comfortable, intimate one-bedroom apartment to experiencing chaos, constriction, and confusion. But by the time I left, we had an administrative structure involving sixty-three people as well as seventy-five different ministry teams led *primarily by the lay members of our congregation*. This book highlights some of the critical structural changes we made, how we went about those changes, and the theological convictions that fueled them.

Stresses, Strains, and Growing Pains

During my twenty years of pulpit ministry, I never doubted the call of God upon my life as a disciple of Jesus Christ and a minister of the gospel. However, I consistently questioned the way we "do" church in my tradition. We "Methodists" have the reputation of having a "method" for doing everything. I am concerned that all too often, we have sanctified our "methods," which were developed for a different time and season of ministry, while constantly changing the "message" we offer the world. In our effort to be all things to all people, we have watered down the essence of the faith while maintaining antiquated structures in their purest (and sometimes most toxic) form.

The genius of John Wesley was the way he connected the distinct message of holiness of heart (justification by faith) and life (sanctification) with methods that touched the unchurched masses of his day (George G. Hunter, *Church for the Unchurched* [Nashville: Abingdon Press, 1996], 66). This combination of "message" and contemporary "methods" sparked the Wesleyan Revival, which ignited England and America for Christ. We already have the message the world needs to hear . . . *but our methods keep getting in the way*.

3

During my pastoral career, I had a growing frustration concerning the methods we use to "do" church. This frustration was twofold and, to some degree, continues today. First, *we have settled for making "church members" and have fallen far short of the Christ-given mission of making "disciples."* We have shifted away from encouraging and helping people to live a lifestyle where Christ-like character is formed in them to practicing a form of religion that gives individuals enough faith to make them socially acceptable, but not enough to empower them to transform the world. We birth spiritual infants, but do little to help them grow to spiritual maturity.

Second, *our structure prohibits us from empowering people for ministry.* This is primarily what this book is about. The church's traditional structure has been a top-down, power-driven, permission-withholding, hierarchical system that has often stifled flexibility or creativity on the part of individuals desiring to minister. For example, if a person actually doing ministry in a local church wanted to try something new, he or she had to get permission from a specific ministry committee ...which then had to get permission from the Council on Ministries... which then had to get permission from the Finance Committee... which then had to get permission from the Administrative Board. Can you sense the frustration (it was frustrating just writing down the sequence)?

At Christ United Methodist Church, many a great ministry idea was vetoed somewhere along the hierarchical pecking order, or the person proposing the idea lost enthusiasm after jumping through all the hoops. I have often joked that a church committee structure is a by-product of the Fall, and that I am grateful God loved the world so much that God sent his Son... and not a committee.

I yearned for a ministry structure that released people to use their God-given distinctiveness in ministry. Even today, I still yearn for churches to adopt a structure that is bottom-up, ministry-driven, permission giving, and collegial. *I believe in the priesthood of all believers.*

I believe, along with Gilbert Bilezikian, that, "Hierarchical structures are ponderous, stifling, and sterile. Flattening them into interconnected small groups and ministry teams holds the only hope for local churches to release the irresistible dynamic of servanthood, and to turn dead or dying institutions into invincible communities of oneness that will devour the world" (Gilbert Bilezikian, *Community 101: Reclaiming the Church as Community of Oneness* [Grand Rapids: Zondervan, 1997], 153). I believe pastors are not called to "do" the ministry, but called to "equip the saints to do the work of ministry" (Ephesians 4:12). Countless people have told me over the years that they never want to serve on another committee because they never *do* anything but only talk about *doing* something. They say, "Please let me be in ministry, but don't make me go to any of those meetings."

Facing these hindrances and convinced there had to be a better, more biblical way to do church, we began to teach, preach, and strategically plan about eight crucial paradigm shifts that needed to take place for our church to be able to fulfill our mission in our postmodern culture (this took place during our first four years together at Christ Church). These shifts were:

1. From thinking of the church as a *religious* organization to seeing the church as a gathering of people trying to be *faithful* in their discipleship to Jesus Christ.
2. From the old image of the *pastor* as the minister to a new image that all our *people* are called and gifted by God to be in ministry.
3. From being a Sunday morning gathering of *acquaintances* to a network of *communities* where people really care for and love one another.
4. From settling for quality that is *adequate*, or good enough, to striving to be *excellent* in all we do for the cause of Christ.
5. From stifling creativity and maintaining traditional responsibility within *committees*, which always tended to withhold permission to try something new, to encouraging creativity and risk taking through semi-autonomously functioning ministry teams that were granted permission to try new ideas and ministries.

6. From serving a slot in ministry out of a sense of *obligation* or duty to discovering where God has gifted each person to serve and doing so out of a sense of *passion*.
7. From the *uniformity* of offering the same old thing to everyone to offering a *variety* of choices for spiritual development and ministry.
8. From settling for making *church members* to being dedicated to the exciting ministry of transforming persons into *fully devoted disciples of Jesus Christ* (Larry F. Beman, "We're Not Playing Church Anymore," *Dateline* [January 1998], 1–3).

As one can imagine, shifting these emphases within our faith community had a dramatic effect on the life and health of our congregation. As people came humbly to the scripture and gained a better understanding of God's heart, we experienced marked growth and a renewed sense of life and vitality. However, during this time of growth, we faced three significant challenges.

First, not everyone caught the vision. For some, the church was a social club of morally clean people that existed to meet the spiritual needs of its members. They had no sense of mission, no burden for those living apart from God, and no desire to help Christ Church transition into a body fit for God's redemptive purposes. Second, our existing structures for facilitating ministry were woefully inadequate. We were assimilating people into ministry positions based on the needs of the church rather than the giftedness of the individual. This led to burnout and overall mediocrity among our ministries. Third, many of our members who were passionate about participating in God's mission had not even heard of the term *postmodernism*, nor were they equipped to engage postmodern nonbelievers for maximum impact. So even as we were experiencing clearer focus, renewal and growth, we were also battling inflexibility, inefficiency, and irrelevance. I'll focus on the first two challenges in this chapter and the third in chapter 2.

People Are Worried

When we started focusing on the eight paradigm shifts listed previously, a fresh burst of energy rippled through the church. Members started inviting friends; the buzz around the community motivated unchurched residents to check us out. From week to week, there were fewer and fewer empty seats in the sanctuary. One day after worship, two couples came through the line and said that they would like to take Beth and me to lunch. I've been around long enough to know that sometimes you're invited to *have* lunch and sometimes you're invited to *be* lunch. I wasn't sure which type of invitation this was but I accepted anyway. Between the ordering of our dinners and the arrival of our appetizer, the conversation went something like this:

"Jeff, thank you for coming to lunch with us today. We want you to know that we love and appreciate you... but we're also here to express a concern that 'people are worried.'"

And our special of the day . . . Roast Greenway comes with rice or potato . . .

Now, I've also been around long enough to know that when people come to me to express concern on behalf of multiple anonymous persons, quite often the most worried of the bunch are standing right in front of me. I began to press them about what "people" were worried about. They shared that the congregation had grown so rapidly and the programs were expanding so quickly that people were worried the congregation was losing its feeling of family. It was growing too fast and they weren't pleased with the results. I asked them why they felt that way, to which they replied, "Well, we just don't know everybody anymore."

I asked a different question: "How many people do you know in the congregation?" They began to list people they knew well until they couldn't think of any more. The number was somewhere around twenty.

I said, "That's interesting. We had ten times that number in worship when I arrived as pastor, but it certainly didn't feel as if we were too big at that time. So let me ask you, why do you know

7

these twenty people so well?" They responded that Sunday school classes, participation in different committees, and opportunities for prayer groups had contributed to their most solid relationships. Upon hearing that, I assured them it was our intent to continue to provide such opportunities for anyone coming to Christ Church. It was our vision to have those kinds of spiritually transforming relationships by offering Sunday school classes, a variety of small groups, and plenty of ministry teams. And when the congregation gathered for worship, even though there would be more people in the worship space, the number of intimate, bonded-together groups within the congregation would also increase. (This was our attempt at implementing John Wesley's understanding of the *ecclesiola* within the *ecclesia*.) We were trying to accommodate our (what we believed to be) God-given growth by emphasizing smaller groups of tightly banded people.

I wish I could tell you that I alleviated, through theological and practical explanation, every concern for those two families, but I didn't. Within eighteen months both couples had left our body. Surprisingly, they did not choose to become a part of a small church but a larger church only two miles down the road. When I pressed them about why they had made this decision that seemed antithetical to the concerns they had raised over lunch, they said they ultimately did not want to go through the hard work of helping the congregation grow and develop. Not to be harsh toward them, but I think they wanted to run a marathon...starting at the twenty-fifth mile marker.

Of course, what those two couples said about Christ Church is true about every congregation engaged in change: *people are worried.* Some will vocalize their worry; others will not. Despite your vision casting, strategic plans, and fresh offerings of programs and opportunities; people will worry that their church is changing in ways that will cost them. Until they learn to die to their own aspirations and agendas for the church, they will constantly wrestle with each change the church makes—even the seemingly minor ones. As Erwin McManus writes, "Any speed of progress looks like blinding speed when everyone else is standing still" (Erwin

Raphael McManus, *Seizing Your Divine Moment: Dare to Live a Life of Adventure* [Nashville: Thomas Nelson, 2002], 234). There's not a whole lot you can do about it, other than be willing to count the cost before you tinker under the hood of the church.

While those couples displayed their fear of change in a mostly passive way (they never caused any real trouble), fear can—and often does—lead to recalcitrant posturing and active resistance. Turf wars can become a reality. Here is an example from a church I served prior to arriving at Christ Church:

In 1985, Beth and I were assigned to First United Methodist Church in Butler, Pennsylvania. The First UMC Butler is a wonderful congregation; in fact, it is the kind of congregation that every pastor should be privileged to serve at one time or another. But the congregation was not without its faults and flaws. During the introductory meeting with the Pastor-Parish Relations Committee, it became very clear that the older women on the committee saw the age and life situation of my wife as a great gift to the congregation. They believed God might have sent her to Butler to be a bridge between their group and the younger women so that the United Methodist Women might be able to reach a new generation.

Shortly after our arrival, Beth began to develop relationships with several of the younger women in the church. They developed a fellowship circle of like-minded young spouses and mothers with similar life concerns. Due to the generational difference between the younger ladies and the older ladies in the church, the expressed and implied *values* were also different. For instance, the younger moms said they would never meet without having some kind of child care. In addition, they agreed to meet at times that were conducive to everyone's schedule. Since some of the younger women worked during the day, the circle decided to meet in the evening.

After a season, the official United Methodist Women's organization contacted Beth about chartering her circle as an official entity of the UMW. After some discussion and the understanding that the larger group would be receptive to some of the lifestyle changes that had occurred from one generation to the next, the younger women decided they would take their place in the ongoing activity of the larger group. They called themselves the Deborah Circle.

Almost immediately, Beth and the other women in Deborah began to notice that some of the generational differences were causing friction. For example, the older women wanted to meet during the day—mostly because that's when they had always met. But for the Deborah women working outside the home, daytime meetings were next to impossible. Secondly, when they did meet, the older women didn't want to contribute to childcare costs so that the Deborah women could attend without scrambling to find a babysitter. Although the younger women had previously expressed that childcare was necessary for them to participate, the older women argued that it was up to the younger women to find child care for themselves.

After several intense negotiation sessions, it was finally agreed that United Methodist Women's meetings would be offered in the day *and* the evening so the younger women could attend. It was also agreed that childcare would be provided during the evening sessions for those who needed it. But the conversation and posturing surrounding those two issues revealed a palpable hesitancy on the part of the older members to change their ways for the good of attracting the younger members.

This particular United Methodist Women's group prided themselves on having several fundraising opportunities during the fall and spring to raise money for mission efforts. Usually these were soup-and-salad or sandwich lunches held each month during the school year. These were very popular events in the life of the community, often attracting people who worked downtown. In addition to exposing all kinds of people to the church, the events consistently helped the UMW meet their pledge for mission efforts every year. After a few years, the Deborah Circle was asked to take their turn in providing the kitchen leadership for one of these soup-and-sandwich lunches. In order to be properly prepared, they were asked to observe the older ladies as they ran one of the luncheons.

Once they arrived, each of them was assigned to an older woman who mentored them through the process of making the soup for the day. Imagine these younger ladies' responses when they discovered that the recipes for the soup were kept in a locked box, and that each recipe had to be followed to the letter. Not wanting to offend, the Deborah women agreed to steadfastly follow the recipe, but a problem arose when the women separated into groups for the purpose of cutting the onions, carrots, and celery for the soup. Each of the Deborah women saw that, after they had cut their particular vegetable, the older woman standing next to them would recut the same piece. When the women began to ask, "Why are you doing that?" one of the older women said, "Well, because you're cutting them wrong."

I don't know if the older women realized what they were saying or how they were being received by the younger women, but as the morning wore on, one by one the younger women put their knives down, said they had something else they needed to do, and left the kitchen. At the end of the morning, Beth was the only Deborah woman left. The older women were convinced that the younger women had forsaken their responsibility and had not completed the task to which they were called. Of course, Beth and I believe that their unwillingness to change *even the way the vegetables were cut* led the younger women to feel unaccepted. The Deborah women of the United Methodist Women's organization never helped in the kitchen again (and few, I am told, have been able to cut vegetables since).

An ironic postscript: over the next several years, that United Methodist Women's group was unable to find the local leadership it needed in order to organize itself for mission and ministry. Within ten years after I left as the pastor of that congregation, the group finally disbanded because they could not find women—older or younger—to come forward in positions of leadership. But after a couple of years, a group of young women came together to form a women's Bible study with a missionary support emphasis. It is now flourishing and making substantial spiritual deposits into the life of that congregation, primarily because they were given the permission to do so in a different way.

So whether changing the atmosphere of a congregation or changing its time-honored traditions, reactions to change take a variety of forms. Inevitably, there will be some people who become so frustrated they end up leaving the church. Fortunately, however, there are some changes that address structural deficiencies and liberate people to live and serve in ways that cause them to forget the discomfort often accompanied by change.

"Congratulations! You've Been Nominated for..."

Another point of stress was the traditional work of the Nominating Committee. In our tradition, this committee (now called the Lay Leadership/Ministry Development Committee) does its work on an annual basis. It is composed of members of the laity, plus the pastors, and usually meets in July to prepare for the annual Charge Conference held in the fall. Its mission, as described in the *1996 Book of Discipline*, is to "nominate to the charge conference or church conference in its annual session such officers and members of the church council, charge conference, and committees as the law of the Church requires or as the conference may determine as necessary to its work" (*The Book of Discipline of The United Methodist Church* [Nashville: The United Methodist Publishing House, 1996], paragraph 262.1, 152).

I came to dread the annual work of our local church's Committee on Nominations and Personnel. The same life-squelching process happened every summer. Twelve reluctant souls would begin the daunting task of filling all the slots called for in our *Book of Discipline* (136–59). Because the process was needs driven, committee participants were seldom as concerned with helping people find their distinct place of service as they were with filling all the slots on the form.

The effect this had on the average church member was under-
standable, and the results were predictable. Some parishioners said
"Yes," and fell into the right place quite by coincidence. Others
said, "Yes," and muddled through each job the church threw at
them year after year, but with little sense of meaning, purpose, or
fulfillment. Such was the life of our church. A by-product of this
system was that the vast majority of folks quickly learned to say,
"No," and refused to serve on traditional boards and committees.
Privately, they would tell me, "I would love to serve in ministry, but
that would mean being on a committee. Committees don't do anything. I want to do something that is going to make a difference."
Or they would say, "I think I would like helping with the church
grounds, but the only call I ever got to serve involved teaching
sixth-grade Sunday school. No thanks." After awhile, people
stopped answering the phone during the annual August/September
onslaught in hopes that the Nominating Committee would find
other warm (or not-so-warm) bodies to fill their slots.

Perhaps I'm exaggerating a little. The point is that, while some
people were able to serve where they were gifted and had passion,
the default result of the Nominating Committee process was that
people ended up "doing time" instead of doing ministry. This problem was (and is) by no means unique to Christ Church. In many
churches, church members are called because the church has a slot
that they need to fill rather than because a person has the gifts,
passion, and style that make for a suitable fit.

A perfect example of this is a young woman (let's call her Darla)
who was identified as a possible candidate for serving in the area
of Children's Ministry. The committee that called her had no idea
she was scared to death of talking with children. In fact, at that
time Darla didn't even know whether or not she wanted to be a
mother someday. Despite the assumption that kids are "easy to
relate to," Darla had difficulty establishing connections with children. Yet they called her because they wanted her to serve as the
Children's Ministry Coordinator and third-grade Sunday school
teacher. She was young, new in the community, and a fresh face
for the Children's Ministry—an attractive demographic.

It was precisely because Darla was new in the community and, thus, eager to be accepted, that she said yes. But it was a comprehensive disaster. The third-grade Sunday school class quickly found out she had no real desire to serve in that particular setting. Personally, Darla felt inadequate, embarrassed, and even resentful toward the committee that called her. Within six months it was clear the committee had made a poor match; that Darla had been slotted into the Children's Ministry because of preconceived notions of how she might be able to serve. Darla plugged on and did her time, but she never said yes to the Nominating Committee again.

Happily, a few years later, Darla grew in her discipleship through participation in an extensive Bible study. As a component of that Bible study, she discovered her particular spiritual gifts, passions, and personal style. Today she is a valued member of a team that collects resources to help the homeless and the hungry in her community. Why does she fit well in this role? For one, she has a heart (passion) for helping those who live far from God and who are broken by the tragedies of our society. Her God-given gifts and passions shine in the midst of pain and bewilderment. Because the Nominating Committee didn't know her—had never asked her about her passions—she was tragically "mis-slotted." Thankfully, she is no longer "doing time," but is, instead, having the most fulfilling time of her life.

Another example of "doing time" is a businessman (we'll call him Curt) who joined a congregation with a Nominating Committee. One year, as the committee was doing its work, somebody said, "Well, Curt's a businessman; let's put him on the Finance Committee." Now, while on the surface it might make sense to have a person who understands banking, who has a good mind for finance, and who has the capacity to read a balance sheet, sit on the Finance Committee, such reasoning ignores the reality of God-given gifts, passions, and personal style. Only when a committee digs under the surface and determines whether the spiritual gifts, passions, and personal style match the opening (regardless of occupational correlation) can they know whether a person is a good fit.

But Curt was slotted in as a member of the Finance Committee anyway. Not long into his tenure, it became apparent that Curt was not able to look at church financial situations through the eyes of faith. It was a constant battle on a month-to-month basis for him to balance the good business sense that he had developed over the years with the ability to take steps and leaps of faith necessary for organizing a church for mission and ministry. After about a year and a half, Curt came to me and said, "Jeff, I don't believe this is a good fit for me, and I hate going to the meetings on a monthly basis. I'd like to find a place where I can get my hands dirty and get myself involved in ministry."

Curt had a passion for creating affordable housing in our community. Shortly after our conversation, we hooked him up with Habitat for Humanity. Today, Curt is retired, is still an active partner in Habitat, and has been involved in building close to two hundred homes in order to provide affordable, reasonable housing for people who most need it. Whether he's doing roof work or handing over the keys to a house's occupants, he's alive in ways he never was when he was on the Finance Committee.

The problem with the traditional way in which our Nominating Committee had worked was that the members of the committee usually didn't have an adequate feel for the entire membership of the congregation. Therefore, they couldn't accurately determine where other members of the Body were gifted and best suited to serve. So, *annually*, we found ourselves calling people we really didn't know to fill slots on the organizational chart of the church—never knowing whether that person had the desire, gifts or skills to do the job well. It is a methodology for mediocrity—*at best*.

Let's illustrate this disconnect a different way. Imagine that you have a 1,000-piece jigsaw puzzle. Would you expect it to fall into place simply by taking the wrapper off the box and shaking its pieces onto the table? Of course not. We all know how to build a puzzle: first you look at the picture on the box. Then you turn the pieces over so that the color side faces up. Then you find all the pieces with a straight edge and begin to piece the border together. Then you begin putting the pieces together using the picture as a guide: each piece . . . in its distinctive place . . . fulfilling its distinctive purpose . . . until the picture on the table is complete and matches the picture on the box. Incidentally, this imagery parallels the New Testament concept of the church being like a human body with each member playing a distinct and important role (1 Corinthians 12). Christ United Methodist Church in Erie, Pennsylvania was a nearly 1,000-piece jigsaw puzzle, and we needed to help each person find his or her God-intended fit for ministry.

God has given *every* congregation *every* gift and grace necessary for *that* congregation to fulfill God's reason for their existence. But most congregations are ineffective in maximizing that opportunity because they don't know how to help people discover their passions, explore their spiritual gifts, and apply them within a distinct ministry niche. Instead, many congregations yearn for the good old days, probably forty or fifty years ago, when they were the only show in town, and all they had to do was open the door of the church building and receive worshipers. I used to joke with the congregations I superintended in Pittsburgh that, while they knew that it was 2003, I was convinced that they went to bed on Saturday night hoping that when they got up on Sunday morning it would be 1953 all over again. They had not been able to adjust who they were and their style of ministry to their context. They placed preferences above calling. That's not far from idolatry.

Other congregations yearn to be like the "other church" down the road. It's an ecclesial form of keeping up with the Joneses. This also is a form of idolatry, but perhaps more a form of covetousness. It's easy to covet another church's location, or denominational support, or responsiveness to vision. But covetousness is still sin, and it obscures the incredible pieces God has already put into any given church.

The biblical reality is that God has distributed people and the gifts as God sees fit according to his purpose and that in every congregation God has the right people in the right place at the right time to do what God wants them to do. The challenge of capitalizing on this reality is threefold:

1. Provide steady leadership that will articulate such a vision;
2. Motivate people to respond to the call God has upon their lives;
3. Implement a system by which people can discover their spiritual gifts and deploy those gifts in a ministry niche that fits their passion and is reflective of their social style.

These concerns will be tackled in chapter 4.

At Christ Church, we also believed each person is called and gifted by God to serve *for a lifetime*—not just a year. Can you imagine what that would be like? Each person...serving in a specific place...fulfilling a distinctive purpose...until the picture that God has in mind for this local expression of the body of Christ begins to come to life? The possibility led us to the conclusion that what we did every year as a Nominating Committee amounted to throwing a puzzle onto a table and expecting that it would miraculously fall together. The question became, how could we help people discover their unique place and niche for service within the body of Christ? There had to be a better way.

Chapters 3–5 in this book will give greater detail as to exactly how we sought that better way, but chapter 2 addresses our first task—a realistic assessment of our cultural context. Although we may not have used *postmodernism* in our day-to-day vocabulary around the church, there were cultural clues that the times were changing. And we had been sticking our heads in the sand for too long with regard to some of those issues. If we were going to be all God intended for us to be at Christ Church, we were going to have to implement the changes we knew we were supposed to make with an eye to postmodernity.

17

❁ ⚜ ❁ ⚜ ❁ ⚜ ❁ ⚜ ❁ ⚜ ❁ ⚜ ❁ ⚜ ❁ ⚜ ❁ ⚜ ❁

CHAPTER TWO

POSTMODERNITY:
THE NEW KID IN THE PEW

As a society, we have been moving from the old to the new. And we are still in motion. Caught between eras, we experience turbulence. Yet, amid the sometimes painful and uncertain present, the restructuring of America proceeds unrelentingly.

With these words, John Naisbitt opens *Megatrends* (New York: Warner Books, 1982, 1), not only describing our country, but also the institutions that form its fabric. Perhaps more frighteningly, he theorizes how our culture will fray and eventually come apart at the seams if our institutions do not stretch and change.

The church of Jesus Christ (and its representative denominations) is certainly one of those institutions. It is also in the process of "moving from the old into the new." Such change is not easy, and the church is experiencing its share of turbulence. Fortunately, this period of church history and change is being analyzed and chronicled by contemporary voices all around us.

For instance, Bill Easum calls this period of rapid change a "crack in history," with technological and societal advances not seen since the invention of the printing press or the industrial revolution (*Sacred Cows Make Gourmet Burgers* [Nashville: Abingdon Press, 1995], 19–29). He makes a compelling case that the church that refuses to change its methods of sharing the unchanging message of the gospel with our ever-changing world will become obsolete and not survive.

Leonard Sweet and Brian McLaren put it this way:

> Many Christians who approach postmodernism as a philosophy misunderstand, oversimplify, and hastily critique it from their vantage point within modernity, not realizing how enmeshed with modernity they are and how much they have made modern culture a cult, and not realizing that their own modernity may well have modified their Christianity more than their Christianity has modified their modernity. (*A Is for Abductive*, 240)

Lesslie Newbigin has chronicled the pluralistic ideology in which the church finds itself today (*The Gospel in a Pluralist Society* [Grand Rapids: William B. Eerdmans, 1989] 222–33). It is no longer viewed as the sole holder and source of truth in our culture. From the world's perspective, the gospel and claims of Christ are only one of several "options" today. Newbigin calls for the church to become a missionary community, a living hermeneutic of the gospel in the world. He states that such a community will have six characteristics:

1. "It will be a community of praise.
2. "It will be a community of truth [in which the canonical story of the gospel is remembered and rehearsed.]
3. "It will be a community that does not live for itself but is deeply involved in its neighborhood.
4. "It will be a community where men and women are prepared for and sustained in the exercise of the priesthood of all believers in the world.
5. "It will be a community of mutual responsibility.
6. "It will be a community of hope."

Newbigin and other mission-minded theologians such as Stanley Hauerwas and William Willimon are calling for the church to clearly establish its identity if it is to make a difference in the world today. (See Stanley Hauerwas and William Willimon, *Resident Aliens: Life in the Christian Colony* [Nashville: Abingdon Press, 1989].)

Loren Mead has also had his finger on the pulse beat of these changing times. Having documented the previous shifts in Christian history (from the Apostolic Era to the Christendom Era to the Enlightenment Era), he makes a case that we are shifting again and that the present structures of the church are "cracking" under the stress of change (something Christ Church didn't just read about; we felt it!). Mead calls for the church to jettison collapsing institutional structures and forms so we may move "ahead into a new paradigm of mission, rebuilding, and reinventing the church as we go" (*The Once and Future Church* [New York: The Alban Institute, 1991] 6, 28-29). He calls for the church to reclaim a clear sense of mission and to throw all its energies and resources behind that mission.

These ecclesial shifts have coincided with and, in some ways, have been precipitated by, the cultural shift known as postmodernity (or postmodernism). Discussing postmodernity in philosophical detail is far beyond the scope of this book. Because postmodernity is still relatively new (when compared with other cultural shifts), it is not wholly definable. However, postmodernity's broader contours are discernable and it's those contours, as well as how they touched upon our life at Christ Church, that have merit for this chapter.

But first a history lesson.

To Rome and Back Again

Many observers agree that there are four major periods of Christian history. Think of it: only *four* in the nearly two thousand years since the beginning of the church of Jesus Christ. The first, the *Apostolic Era*, began in AD 33 with the death, resurrection, and ascension of Jesus Christ, as well as the gift of the Holy Spirit being poured out on all flesh at Pentecost. It lasted for a little under three hundred years until about AD 313. This, as the New Testament reveals, was the church in its earliest, most basic form. In the Bible and in history, the church of this age was a minority sect in a pluralistic, pagan culture.

To become a follower of Jesus in this era was a life-altering decision. Followers of Jesus were labeled enemies of Judaism *and* Rome. The ministry emphasis of the early church was a holistic form of evangelism. Billy Abraham has described this as "the primary initiation into the kingdom of God" (William J. Abraham, *The Logic of Evangelism* [Grand Rapids: William B. Eerdmans, 1989], 13). There is strong evidence of personal and corporate evangelism, catechesis (or disciple-making), distribution of spiritual gifts among the followers of Jesus for mission and ministry, and engaging the entire body of Christ in its primary mission of making disciples. The Apostolic church was formed around the priesthood of all believers . . . the *Laos* . . . the whole people of God.

The Apostolic church was more an organism than it was an organization. While later New Testament writings refer to deacons, elders, and even bishops, the church doesn't seem to be structure-oriented, but rather leadership-oriented, in order to align the church's use of the gifts of ministry for the rest of the body of Christ (see Ephesians 4, Romans 12, and 1 Corinthians 12). Followers of Jesus met in homes for prayer, worship, and fellowship. These weren't structured offerings from the church, courtesy of the Small Group or Prayer Ministries; this was how they were the church.

The Apostolic church was a first-generation church that lived beyond self-interest. They were a contagious, evangelistic, disciple-making, mission-hearted community of faith. That's the kind of church we read about in the New Testament.

The second major era of the Christian faith is called the *Christendom Era*. It started around AD 313, when the Roman Emperor Constantine was converted to Christ. Subsequent to his conversion, he made Christianity the official religion of Rome. Church and State began to function as one and the same. The Church became the primary shaper of the mores of the culture. But as Christianity became more and more mainstream, the emphasis on evangelism and disciple making began to wane. People no longer became Christians because they left a former way of life to join a counter-cultural movement; they, instead, became Christians because they were born into the "Christendom" culture. Christendom became a social, economic, and political way of life with Church and State working hand in hand. (If you drive through Middle America, you can see a clear sign of the residue of Christendom. When you go to a county seat, take a look at the town square. On one end of the town square will be the county courthouse. What's on the other end? A church. And if you research the history of that town, the players in the county courthouse were likely also the players in that church. The pastor of that congregation was often the most influential person in the community. Church and State functioned together. They determined what happened in that community. Church and State, working together, was Christendom at its zenith.)

As a result, the Church began to move away from the Great Commission mission as described in the New Testament, in favor of a codification and ritualization of the Christian life from cradle to grave. In the Christendom tradition, seven different sacraments were developed to mark the journey from cradle to grave: baptism, confession, communion, confirmation, marriage, ordination, and last rites.

During this era, the Christian Church became institutionalized. The Church erected cathedrals and developed administrative structures to preserve the institution. The Church also developed a highly sophisticated stratification of clergy leadership with less emphasis placed upon the priesthood of all believers. Not surprisingly, spiritual gifts are rarely mentioned in the writings of this era. Pastors/priests became the mediators of grace and held the functions of ministry within their office. They became the sole interpreters of Scripture and the dispensers of grace through the sacraments. The work of the people . . . the *Laos* . . . was relegated to attending worship, giving the offering, receiving the sacraments, and doing the liturgy of the Church. Also, the foundational doctrines of the Apostolic Era began to be interpreted and codified into the dogma of the Christendom Church.

The third era of Christian history is the *Modern/Enlightenment Era*. It started about 1750 with the rise of the Industrial Revolution and the Academy. At the beginning of this era, Church and State worked together, as is evidenced in Wesley's England and the early history of the United States. But as the Enlightenment began to take root, skepticism and rationalism flourished. The long-held doctrines and dogmas of the Christendom Era were called into question. Eventually, the Church began to lose its sway over the State.

Skepticism also altered the way many viewed the Scriptures. The authority of Scripture was compromised. The miracles were questioned. The sinful condition of humanity was rationalized. The divinity and resurrection of Jesus were diminished to a fable. The result? Without the authority of Scripture and the divinity of Jesus, without the power and reality of the resurrection, the Christian faith of the Enlightenment became a collection of moral teachings that, in the words of Wesley, "had the form of religion, but lacked the power."

The Church began to question whether the foundations of our faith were true, and as that became the norm, it began to lose its place of privilege in the culture. For the last two hundred years, the church of Jesus has been an institutional organization in survival mode . . . rather than a vital organism.

This brings us back to the emphasis of this chapter: the *Postmodern Era*—or, the fourth age of church history. This is the era we're living in right now and it looks like *the first century all over again*. The Christian church, whether we choose to realize it or not, is once again a minority sect in a prevailingly pluralistic, pagan world culture. And here's the kicker: I think it's outstanding. Let's not weep for Christendom's passing or long for the happy marriage of Church and State. Let's be glad and excited that we live in this Post-Christendom, Post-Enlightenment, postmodern era.

For the church to be relevant in the present and in the future, the answer is in our past. We need to pick up the mantle of the

Apostolic church, to be distinctively who we are, to call people to life change and transformation, to become intentional about personal and corporate evangelism, to model *catechesis* (disciple making), to emphasize the discovery and use of spiritual gifts among the followers of Jesus for mission and ministry, and to engage the whole people of God in the critical mission of making disciples.

Because the postmodern age reflects many of the dynamics of the Apostolic Church age, an amazing thing is happening today—almost as if God has pulled back the screen of Scripture and enabled us to rediscover the spiritual gifts all over again. During the last couple of decades, clergy leaders have begun to rise up and say, "I'm not the only one to do ministry here, but I'm to help you, to equip you to do the work of ministry for building up the body of Christ in the manner of Ephesians 4." For the church to live and flourish in this era, it must once again become a counter-cultural movement. We're not supposed to look like the world—we're supposed to look distinctively different from the world and call people to a different kind of life. That holds true not only morally—which is where so much of the Christendom emphasis went—but ecclesially as well. We can't do church in the same manner as a Fortune 500 company.

But perhaps the largest ecclesial problem, as we pass from one age into the next, is the responsiveness of the church. Culturally, the church is viewed as the minority sect within a pagan, pluralistic culture, but *we keep trying to operate as though we live in Christendom.* We spend all of our energy maintaining organizational structures rather than being an organism that penetrates the world. We spend our energy trying to make members who become a part of our club rather than making disciples of Jesus Christ with a kingdom view. We train clergy leaders who hold power and see themselves as the sole dispensers of grace rather than as fellow pilgrims on the journey whose role is to call people to faith, equip them for ministry, and to set them free to minister to others in Jesus' name.

In some ways, this is what happened at Christ Church. Postmodernity was the new kid in the pew and no one wanted to engage it. As we discussed the need to retool many of our structures and approaches, it was clear that the resistance to change had its roots in an unspoken loyalty to Christendom. There was an ache for the status quo—the "good old days"— that hindered mission and reinforced exclusivity. But if any church is to live, we must remember what time it is. We are not in Christendom anymore. The Enlightenment is running out its course. Some may be dismayed about the milieu of this context, but not me. This is a great time to be a part of the kingdom. In the words of Hauerwas and Willimon:

> For us, the world has ended. We may have thought that Jesus came to make nice people even nicer, that Jesus hoped to make a democratic Caesar just a bit more democratic, to make the world a bit better place for the poor. The Sermon, however, collides with such accommodationist thinking. It drives us back to a completely new conception of what it means for people to live with one another. That completely new conception is the church. All that we have heard said of old is thrown up for grabs, demands to be reexamined, and pushed back to square one. Square one is that colony made up of those who are special, different, alien, and distinctive only in the sense that they are those who have heard Jesus say "Follow me," and have come forth to be part of a new people, a colony formed by hearing his invitation and saying yes. (*Resident Aliens*, 92)

Don't get me wrong; I am grateful that Christianity influenced the course of human civilization for more than ten centuries. But it was a relaxed Christianity. It was institutionally controlled and lacked the risk-it-all-for-Jesus mentality employed by the pre-Constantinian church. Church history, beginning with the book of Acts, tells us that the church actually grew in *hostile conditions*. As followers of Jesus faced high stakes for their commitment to their Lord, more and more people were added. People began to live for something worth dying for. The church lived and witnessed with a potency that was lost during the docile age of Christendom. The church, again, is faced with a turbulent cultural environment in this postmodern era. *Which is all the more reason we desperately need a rediscovery of what it means to be the church within this cultural context.*

Speaking at a large meeting on evangelism, sociologist and market researcher George Barna chronicled the cultural shifts that have left the church behind. He gave compelling statistical information describing a church that has largely syncretized aspects of various spiritualities into a generic faith called "Christianity," but this faith hardly resembles the Jesus of the Bible. Barna observed that postmodern culture has rejected moral absolutes given in the Bible, and that those who want to make evangelism relevant today must contextualize their ministry while guarding against losing the truth entrusted to their stewardship (from lectures delivered at the 1999 Congress on Evangelism of The United Methodist Church in New Orleans, LA).

While many Christians are lamenting and pining for the happy days of Christendom (with *happy* meaning "comfortable"), true disciples are getting on with the tasks of engaging the new world, remembering the adage: "The good old days weren't really all that good."

A Change in Mind-set

Let me say that I am *not* advocating wholesale allegiance to postmodernity. I am devoted to Jesus Christ, not a philosophical or cultural swell. The church in the Apostolic Age revolutionized Judea, Samaria, and beyond without selling itself to Roman-Hellenism. We must be wise in the way we approach this postmodern age. Long before postmodernity, E. Stanley Jones wrote: "If the church of this age marries the spirit of this age, then in the next generation it will be a widow. For this generation of secularism will be succeeded by another generation of secularism with its culture and its language and its outlook. For secularism has no fixed basis; it is the result of drives that ebb and flow and go the way of pressures" (Eunice Jones Mathews and James K. Mathews, comp., *Selections from E. Stanley Jones: Christ and Human Need*, [Nashville: Abingdon Press, 1972], 81). Jones is right that secularism has no fixed basis; but the church *does* and that basis is Jesus Christ! His words and his character direct his church to accomplish his mission in the world.

That said, *because of postmodernity*, the church has to adapt its strategy for carrying out Jesus' mission. We can't pretend there hasn't been a shift from The Enlightenment/Modern Age to Postmodernity. It's happened, and the church needs to understand that ignoring postmodernity is not faithfulness to the gospel—it is faithfulness to Christendom.

Thus, the changes we needed to make at Christ Church were changes influenced by postmodernity. In this way, through what I call a "Christian handling," postmodernity served the church. This cultural shift alerted us to ways in which we were more faithful to Christendom than to Jesus' vision for the church.

One such needed change was the shift from settling for "making church members" to being intentional about "making disciples" of Jesus Christ. This is a clear difference between Christendom (which was about "being in") and a Christian handling of postmodernity (which emphasizes authenticity and mission). To show the qualitative difference between the two, consider this quote from E. Stanley Jones, describing his conversion as a youth:

> I climbed over the young men, went down the steps and up the aisle to the altar, and took my place among the seekers. I felt undone and wept—wept because I was guilty and estranged. I fumbled for the latchstring of the Kingdom of God, missed it, for they didn't tell me the steps to find. I stood up at the close when they asked if it was all right with us. I wanted the Kingdom of God, wanted reconciliation with my heavenly Father, but took church membership as a substitute. (*A Song of Ascents* [Nashville: Abingdon Press, 1968], 26)

A church member is comfortable in a church where the pastor does all the work. A disciple sees that Jesus was regularly in the mix of messy ministry and wants to do likewise. A church member brings a consumer mentality with all the trappings. A disciple surrenders him or herself and concentrates on the mission of the church—*why it exists.* A church member hopes the non-Christian will either "get saved" or simply go away. A disciple is devoted to ministering to all people in context.

So for Christ Church, the challenge was to help people convert from a mind-set that saw "joining the church" as mental agreement to a set of doctrines and faithful attendance to a mind-set of joining a body of believers for the purpose of mission. This, as you would imagine, caused more than a few sparks to fly.

Another shift we needed to make was from the Modern/Enlightenment approach to evangelism to a more relational (and less informational) approach. Craig Miller, a staff member of the General Board of Discipleship, wrote an interesting analysis of the generation being raised in this postmodern culture. He quotes Tim Celek, pastor of Calvary-Newport Mesa Church in California, which has been effective at stimulating spiritual dialog with postmodern non-Christians. According to Miller: "[Celek] says that in order to attract and retain Postmoderns the church must offer the most attractive alternative" to what we instinctively think of as evangelism.

> Instead of standing on the street corner and proclaiming that we have the truth, the local church must create a place of integrity, compassion, and authenticity in which Postmoderns can find a safe place to seek God. [Celek] is convinced that once Postmoderns discover the power and excitement of the Christian alternative they will find the truth through faith in Jesus Christ. (Craig Kennet Miller, *Postmoderns: The Beliefs, Hopes and Fears of Young Americans (1965–1981)* [Nashville: Discipleship Resources, 1996], 167)

This is a dramatically different understanding of the evangelistic task than what has traditionally prevailed in most churches.

Older models tended to be more didactic in approach. They largely operated on the assumption that if we would just confront people with the truth of the gospel, they would have no choice but be convicted of sin, see the need for a Savior, and invite Jesus into their hearts and lives as Savior and Lord. After years of evidence to the contrary, it is still difficult to convince people who bank on these models.

Agreeing with Celek, George Barna (1999 lectures) says the evangelism models that are most effective in the postmodern era are more Socratic in their approach. They involve inviting persons outside the community of faith into true friendship, authentic Christian community, and conversations about God in which their questions are engaged with respect. No doubt, these kinds of conversations can get sticky, confusing, heated, or downright irreverent (see Donald Miller, *Blue Like Jazz: Nonreligious Thoughts on Christian Spirituality* [Nashville: Thomas Nelson, 2003]); but these conversations about God (including the doubts and questions of the seeker) invite folks onto the journey of faith and are one of the evidences of the prevenient grace of God in their lives. As N.T. Wright says:

> How are you to address this world with the gospel of Jesus? You cannot just hurl true doctrine at it. You will either crush people or drive them away . . . The answer to the challenge of postmodernism is not to run back tearfully into the arms of modernism. It is to hear in postmodernity God's judgment on the follies and failings, the sheer selfish arrogance, of modernity and to look and pray and work for the resurrection into God's new world out beyond. We live at a great cultural turning point; Christian mission in the postmodern world must be the means of the church grasping the initiative and enabling our world to turn the corner in the right direction. (*The Challenge of Jesus: Rediscovering Who Jesus Was and Is* [Downers Grove: InterVarsity Press, 1999], 167–68)

Whatever methodology we adopt, it will have to be able to adapt to our context without compromising the essence of our faith. In his book, *The Logic of Evangelism*, Billy Abraham has done an excellent job laying the theological foundation for such a process. Defining evangelism as "primary initiation into the kingdom of God" (Abraham, *The Logic of Evangelism*, 13), he highlights six key elements or essential activities in this process of initiation:

1. Conversion and new birth in Christ.
2. Physical incorporation into the church through baptism.
3. Training initiates in the morality of loving God and loving neighbor.
4. Training initiates in the substance of the Christian creed.
5. Introducing initiates to the gifts of the Spirit and equipping them for ministry.
6. Providing initiates with the basic rudiments of the classical spiritual disciplines. (142)

Abraham asserts that spiritual miscarriages are a common feature of a modern evangelism that depends solely on the proclamation method in which "the evangelist preaches . . . the seed is sown and takes root within the womb, significant nourishment is supplied from the bloodstream of the mother church, but then the food is cut off or crucial genetic material for the structuring of the new life is not given. The results are predictable: the developing embryo is aborted, or, if it comes to birth, it is weak and malformed" (140). The process Abraham calls for provides the experiential, communal, and moral dimensions of initiation, and the intellectual, operational, and disciplinary aspects of our faith (see 142). It provides the nutrition and training to help initiates grow from spiritual infancy to Christian maturity.

I'd like to say Christ Church recognized the trends in evangelism, but we did not. As a result, most people thought of evangelism as "winning people to Christ" in a decisive moment, rather than the long, slow, and often-detoured road of conversation and challenge. Thankfully, there are many products available to help churches in transition utilize more effective methods of evangelism to postmoderns. (See Garry Poole, *Seeker Small Groups:*

Engaging Spiritual Seekers in Life-Changing Discussions [Grand Rapids: Zondervan, 2003].)

Postmodernism is akin to a cussword in most church circles, and it poses its challenges. But faithful churches will refuse to retreat from it, believing that Jesus has more than equipped his church to accomplish his mission in any cultural context. Understanding our culture prepares us to use our God-given spiritual gifts in creative and intelligent ways.

CHAPTER THREE

THEOLOGICAL CONVICTIONS
ON THE ROAD TO CHANGE

Any time we want to bring about change, we must take two critical steps. First, we must create or acknowledge dissatisfaction with what exists. And second, we must create a vision of what the future can look like. Both steps take constant communication and teaching. It can't be done in any other way. Unless a pastor commits to do that, he's not going to change anything.
—E. Glenn Wagner, Escape from Church, Inc.

History is replete with the records of faithful people who have sacrificed courageously in order for the gospel to continue to be relevant. For example, the Apostle Paul followed his calling to be a missionary to the Gentiles and for the first time in the history of the Christian movement, the gospel was taken to people outside the Jewish community. This was indeed risky, but his faithfulness made it possible for Gentiles to receive the good news of Jesus Christ.

More recently in church history, an Anglican priest named John Wesley found that the church in which he was ministering was lifeless. It had all the form of religion but lacked the power. Through the practice of spiritual disciplines and deepening his faith in small-group ministry, Wesley began to do revolutionary things that turned the Anglican Church in his day upside down and birthed the Methodist movement. The embers of the

33

Methodist movement came across the Atlantic Ocean to the Colonies in America, fanned into flame, and began to spread like wildfire across the American frontier.

One of the unique things about the Methodist movement spawned by John Wesley is that preachers were willing to preach the gospel anywhere and at any time. Wesley was seen as a renegade for his outdoor preaching. In reality, he was taking the gospel to people who needed to hear it most. That was one of the attractive things about the Methodist message when it came to America. The circuit-riding preachers did not depend upon the assignment of a church to put them in a preaching post; instead, they went from town to town and established preaching posts, class meetings, and societies that soon flourished into congregations. These congregations became the fabric and backbone upon which much of the spiritual life of America was built during its first centuries.

Today's examples of those who have made courageous steps for change include congregations that have offered or switched entirely to alternative worship styles, congregations that have integrated a passion for souls with compassion for people by making sure that social justice is knit into the fabric of the congregation's ministries, congregations that have decided to abandon a setting where people no longer live in order to relocate and expand the scope of ministry, congregations that have added a worship celebration that meets the needs of a different indigenous group that has become a part of the community, and finally, congregations that have not been afraid to stand up for truth while *simultaneously* seeking to understand postmodernity and its implications for the local church.

Several years ago, I had the opportunity of visiting Culmore United Methodist Church in Falls Church, Virginia. Culmore was being pastored by a doctoral student from Wesley Theological Seminary in Washington, D.C. and was located in a community that had experienced "white flight" twenty years prior. It was now in the midst of the most culturally diverse zip code in the United States of America. In that congregation, there were forty-three different groups of varying national heritages, and forty-three different languages that might be spoken on any given Sunday morning. Aware of the unique dynamics, this congregation made a radical decision to no longer *do* church the way it had been done in the 1950s. Instead, they would use their diversity as a strength and find a way to "be" church in the 1990s and beyond. The pastor of that congregation found there were two crucial needs that would influence whether or not they could make such a transition. The first was the need for English as a second language and the second was a deep desire to know and love Jesus Christ. They built upon English as a second language as the delivery platform for the mission and ministry. The congregation began to flourish as a multicultural, multinational, multilingual community based upon those two common loves—the love of learning English as a second language and the love of knowing and living in response to Jesus Christ. That congregation found its niche and regained its vitality only because it was willing to change

In chapter 1, I outlined a few of the *internal* factors that were hindering us from reaching our full potential. In chapter 2, I pointed to a major *external* factor in the cultural shift to postmodernity, which challenged us to change. In this chapter, I want to share five foundational theological and practical convictions that pushed us to change at Christ Church. Then, I will describe our understanding of spiritual gifts going into the change process.

Theology and Ethics: Moving toward Ephesians 4:12

Change never happens in a vacuum. It is always a response to internal or external factors. While Christ Church was hamstrung with the committee structure, anemic from the nomination process, and mired in the relational fisticuffs of turf wars, as well as walking around like aliens in this new world of postmodern thought, we were coming afresh to the Bible and gaining deeper theological insight into God's design for organizing the church. This led to intense questioning regarding how we were doing church and how we could do it, not just *better* but biblically. Here were our five foundational theological convictions and applications regarding Scripture's teaching on church organization.

Spiritual Gifts and the Ministry of the Church

I have done much research into the history and theology of *the charismata*. I am aware of the competing theories and theologies about their reality, viability, and use, but agree with Bruce Bugbee that "spiritual gifts are divine abilities distributed by the Holy Spirit to every believer according to God's design and grace for the common good of the body of Christ" (*What You Do Best in the Body of Christ* [Grand Rapids: Zondervan, 1995], 52). Spiritual gifts are normative for the operation of the church.

These are exciting days to be a part of God's work in the world. The charismatic renewal movement of the 1950s and 1960s reintroduced the church to the spiritual gifts after nearly two millennia of relative silence. Subsequent years have moved the gifts of the Holy Spirit from the fringe of the church into a place of relative respectability. At every level, persons are rediscovering that a healthy understanding and experience of the gifts of the Holy Spirit are crucial keys to understanding the ministry and function of the church.

The "priesthood of all believers," rediscovered over four hundred years ago by Martin Luther, is being reemphasized, and it has the potential to alter the landscape of the church during this postmodern era. Clergy are discovering ministry is not something they do alone; rather they are to train and equip *all* the members of the body of Christ to discover and use their spiritual gifts in a shared ministry. In those places where gifts are being discovered and ministry is being shared, the church is growing in both numbers and effective ministry that are similar to the Apostolic Age.

In the New Testament, the Greek word usually used for spiritual gifts is *charismata*. It is generally agreed that there are four *primary* texts referring to these gifts found in the New Testament (for example, see Charles V. Bryant, *Rediscovering the Charismata* [Waco: Word Books, 1986], 62):

- Romans 12:6-8
- 1 Corinthians 12:8-11, 28
- Ephesians 4:6-8, 11-14
- 1 Peter 4:10-11

There are also secondary passages referring to the spiritual gifts (see Kenneth Cain Kinghorn, *Gifts of the Spirit* [Abingdon Press, 1976], 22), including:

- 1 Corinthians 1:5-7; 12:29-30; 13:8
- 2 Corinthians 8:7
- 1 Thessalonians 5:20
- 1 Timothy 4:14
- 2 Timothy 1:6-7
- Hebrews 2:4

Ken Kinghorn has concluded that these primary and secondary passages taken together yield five basic biblical principles regarding the *charismata*. These principles keep spiritual gifts in proper perspective—encouraging humility and refusing to give pride a foothold (see 22–30):

1. *"God imparts spiritual gifts according to his divine grace; they cannot be earned by human merit."* Most of our parishioners are taught to think upward. They labor, acquire skills, earn promotions, labor some more, receive opportunities, and become more and more marketable. This is antithetical to the life of the church. According to 1 Corinthians 12:11, "All these [gifts] are activated by one and the same Spirit, who allots to each one individually just as the Spirit chooses."

God, through God's Holy Spirit, imparts spiritual gifts. One's education, work history, or training has little or nothing to do with how God arranges the gifts within the body. It is true that God often honors the raw materials of a person he has shaped through various experiences, but a correlation between the two should not be expected.

2. *"God gives spiritual gifts according to his own discretion; God is not bound by man's wishes."* This is a corollary to the above point. A person may desire to have the gift of leadership. He or she may read books on leadership, attend leadership seminars, and ask veteran pastors questions about leadership. But if God, in his sovereign wisdom, arranges for that individual to be gifted with knowledge—the role of a scholar—no amount of leadership training will cause him or her to "acquire" the gift of leadership.

3. *"God wills that every Christian exercise spiritual gifts; these divine enablings are not limited to a few believers."* God's design for the church works against almost every paradigm we are familiar with in contemporary society. In high school, only the best twelve basketball players make the varsity basketball team. In college, only the top students earn scholarships. At work, only the best of the best earn promotions. As a result, those who aren't as smart, talented, or athletic watch as the top performers shine in the spotlight. Not in the church, which means . . . everybody gets a gift. "To *each* is given the manifestation of the Spirit for the common good" (1 Corinthians 12:7). Everybody has a role. "The members of the body that seem to be weaker are indispensable" (1 Corinthians 12:22). Everybody gets to play. The church cannot, and was never intended to, rely on professionals to do the work of ministry. And in this postmodern era, where institutions are suspect and those with power are almost inherently distrusted, even *attempting* to minister without the full complement of saints in shared ministry will spell disaster.

4. *"God provides gifts for the purpose of ministry and service; they are not given in order to draw attention to man or to satisfy his*

ego." Are you starting to detect a pattern in Kinghorn's biblical theology of spiritual gifts? It's not about you. "To each is given the manifestation of the Spirit for the common good" (1 Corinthians 12:7). For the common good—not for ego gratification or aspirations of grandiosity. The church is gifted for the purpose of giving itself away.

In 1 Corinthians 12:14-24, Paul seems to address two kinds of thinking. The first imaginary group seems to have felt inadequate because their gifts were less visible than others. Paul confirms that everybody is necessary in the body. The second group seems to have to looked down on those in the first group, leading Paul to say, "The eye cannot say to the hand, 'I have no need of you,' nor again the head to the feet, 'I have no need of you'" (1 Corinthians 12:21). As the Corinthian church shows, ego desires and spiritual gifts are a potentially combustible combination, causing a nasty concoction of inferiority and arrogance.

5. *"God intends that the ministry of the church be accomplished through spiritual gifts; human talents are not adequate for spiritual ministry."* There is something powerfully distinctive about the New Testament/Apostolic church as evidenced in the canonical record and history. This community exhibited vital expressions of effective ministry, structured only by the free and directive power of the Holy Spirit. Under the Holy Spirit's directing and gifting, the church was a highly visible community made up of complementary and supplementary parts, which were distinctively and functionally different. Surely, their effectiveness and power was due to their exercise of spiritual gifts. To repeat Kinghorn's final thought: *"human talents are not adequate for spiritual ministry."*

Preparation for a Lifetime of Service

Since we believed that every believer has been called and gifted by God for service in God's Kingdom—for life—we concluded that the traditional way in which the Nominating Committee had done its work does not adequately train people for a *lifetime* of service.

Not only is this traditional approach not effective in helping people serve where they are gifted, it tends to foster the perception that ministry is only a limited season in a believer's life. It's true that some ministries have a limited life span, but we are called and gifted by God for a *lifetime* of service. Check the Gospels. Check the letters of Paul, Peter, John, and the other New Testament authors: There is no retiring from the church. Once you become a ligament that supports the body in doing its work, you can't remove yourself from service without damaging the body. Love of God and love of neighbor expressed through spiritual gifts for the good of others is a lifetime contract. I was appointed to Christ United Methodist Church in 1992. One of the first persons that I met was Judy Nass (Judy's story is used by permission). Judy is a person with special needs who has worked her entire life to overcome handicaps that would have caused lesser people to stay in a shell of self-pity and defeat. Judy came to life in our congregation and today still lives for her service to Christ.

Unfortunately, Judy would never say no to a request. When I began to walk through the Nominating Committee process of that congregation during my first year, I noticed that Judy's name appeared on the nominating report in at least ten different places. I also knew enough about the ministry of the congregation to know she really wasn't functioning optimally in any of those places. Rather, there were places where she felt called and gifted to serve; yet she ended up serving in other ministries because she felt an obligation to "do her time."

I scheduled a pastoral call to go and visit Judy. After a brief conversation where I expressed appreciation for her service, she shared with me that she was afraid I was there to tell her she wasn't going to be allowed to serve in the church anymore (she knew she was ineffective where she had been placed). I assured her that was not my intent. Instead, I wanted to help her find an area of service where she would thrive. I said, "Judy, what are one or two areas where you feel you are called and gifted to serve—the kind of places that give you life and energy?" She said that without fail it was her role as the financial secretary of the church as well as the treasurer for the missions organization. I said, "What would happen if I were to just let you do those two things and release you from the other eight?" Her face lit up and she said, "That would be a gift to me."

Now some pastors might think, *"But what about the other eight?"* I was sure that thought was rolling around in the back of Judy's mind, so I said, "Judy, from now on you are going to do these two jobs and all the others that you have been listed to do we'll find somebody else to do them or else we'll decide as a congregation that that is not what God is calling us to do right now." Judy was elated. To this day, I hear from her about once a month by mail or e-mail; she constantly tells me about how fulfilling those two roles are in her life, how much she loves the church and her Lord, and how being released from eight jobs was an important part of her spiritual growth.

In an age where doing the work of ministry was understood as "doing time," we had a hard road ahead of us. Still, we attempted to develop a high-commitment congregation where people could discover where they were "Gifted to Serve" and do so for a lifetime.

The Requirements of
Authentic Ministry and Mission

Building upon the previous two beliefs—*gifts are normative for the operation of the church; God calls us to a lifetime of service*—we also understood that *the priesthood of all believers calls for a shift in the way we have historically organized our churches for mission and ministry.* When I went to seminary, I was trained in accordance with the German model of equipping pastors to be a theologian-in-residence—the "answer-guy." I was equipped to answer secular society's toughest questions about the faith. In addition to this, I was also trained to be the central nervous system of the church—knowing everything that happened in the church, from who was in charge of a given potluck to who could volunteer to cut the church grass.

These days are (mercifully) over. In this postmodern era, clergy and laity share ministry, recovering the biblical way to carry out the work of the church. In fact, we are slowly returning to the New Testament model of leaders using their gifts "to equip the saints [the rest of the church] for the work of ministry, for build-ing up the body of Christ..." (Ephesians 4:12). As followers discover their gifts, they recognize that God has provided specifi-cally gifted leaders to direct them in the work.

When Martin Luther started the Protestant Reformation close to five hundred years ago, he did so on the basis of three primary tenets. The first was *sola scriptura,* that the Scriptures alone, the sixty-six books of the Old and New Testaments, are the sufficient rule of faith and practice. Martin Luther labored to strip away the doctrine and dogma of the Roman Catholic Church that had pre-vented people from experiencing the movement of the Holy Spirit in the hearts and lives of the people. He diligently pushed the Protestant reformers back to the basics of the Scriptures.

The second tenet of the Protestant Reformation was *sola fidei;* human beings are saved by faith alone. The church in Luther's day permitted the sale of indulgences for the forgiveness of sin and entrance into heaven. Luther abhorred this corruption, proclaim-ing that salvation was not something to be bought or earned, but rather comes by faith in Jesus Christ.

The last tenet was the priesthood of all believers, in which all persons are called and gifted to serve in the body of Christ for the ministry of the church. It is interesting to me that the early Protestant movement readily embraced the first two tenets, but it has taken nearly five hundred years for the priesthood of all believers to come full circle. God has revealed through Scripture, after years of ignorance, the truth and profundity of the spiritual giftedness of people. Contemporary writers on the ministry of the laity usually agree that the Reformation delivered to the people an authoritative and accessible Scripture, as well as the theological tenet of justification by grace through faith alone—but failed to deliver on its promise of the priesthood of all believers (see Greg Ogden, *The New Reformation: Returning the Ministry to the People of God* [Grand Rapids: Zondervan, 1990], 11). It appears we are living in the era when the unfinished business of the Reformation may be completed. This shift will dramatically alter the way churches organize themselves for mission and ministry.

Systems Theory Works

Systems theory is the simple idea that a "system is designed for the results it is getting. If you want different results, you will have to redesign the system" (Ezra Earl Jones, *Quest for Quality in the Church: A New Paradigm* [Nashville: Discipleship Resources, 1993], vi). If you don't like the results of the ministry of the church, then you need to adjust or change the system in order to produce the desired effects. When we thoughtfully analyzed the system we were using to operate Christ Church, we came to a sobering conclusion: The system we utilized for years was effective at maintaining the status quo and making church members; it fell far short of our desire to develop a dynamic community of faith that would produce passionate disciples of Jesus Christ.

Jim Collins writes in his best-selling book, *Good to Great*, something that not only makes sense for companies, but rings true in the church as well: "the purpose of bureaucracy is to compensate for incompetence and lack of discipline—a problem that largely goes away if you have the right people in the first place" (New York: HarperBusiness, 2001, 121). We had a system loaded with bureaucracy, supposedly so that the church would work efficiently and effectively. Instead, it had the opposite effect; it bogged down any budding ministry with tentacles of tedium. What Collins is saying about companies is what 1 Corinthians 12, Romans 12, and Ephesians 4 say about the church: if the right people are in the right places, *you don't need bureaucracy*.

However a church goes about doing the work of ministry, some kind of system or methodology is involved. We junked our old system and began to focus on the uniqueness and giftedness of Christ-followers as our method for doing ministry. We didn't miss the bureaucracy one bit. Would you?

Change Is Slow and Painful

This reality alone causes many churches to sit on their best ideas for change. There is no glossing over the fact that change is difficult. But if managed in a positive way, the strains and stresses produced during that awkward time will pay off in the end. Our leadership team worked under the assumption that navigating change would be an opportunity for us to discover a new dimension of God's will for our congregation. However, we also knew that people react to change differently, and that we needed to be patient as individuals slowly adopted our new model for ministry.

In his book, *Diffusion of Innovation* (4th ed. [New York: The Free Press, 1995], 262–66), Everett M. Rogers breaks down the acceptance of change in any group (including a congregation) into five distinct phases or groups:

1. "Innovative Leaders" (2.5%) are the adventuresome risk takers in any group. These folks have a high capacity to deal with uncertainty and change, are always looking for and thinking of new ways to do things, and tend to be willing to try almost anything.
2. "Opinion Leaders" (13.5%) are the early adopters of innovative ideas. They are well respected and are perceived as role models whose opinion matters. They make judicious decisions and discretely use new ideas
3. "Early Majority" (34%) pertains to the next wave of acceptance in any organization. They are well connected in the organization, but are not perceived to be opinion leaders. They take longer to make decisions about new

innovations, and they usually take their lead from the Opinion Leaders. Their life motto is "Be not the first by which the new are tried, / Nor yet the last to lay the old aside" (Alexander Pope, *An Essay on Criticism*).

4. "Late Majority" (34%) is the fourth group of people who embrace change. These folks tend to be skeptical, often feeling threatened by new ideas. They adopt only after the majority has embraced the change. The people in this group cannot handle a high degree of uncertainty, so the leader must map things out very clearly and simply for them.

5. Last Adopters or "Laggards" (16%) are the lowest risk takers in any organization. They have little if any influence, and are suspicious of new ideas and those promoting them. They tend to be nostalgic, yearning for the good old days, and are the proponents of the *seven last words of the church:* "We never did it that way before."

At Christ Church, our momentum increased when the Opinion Leaders, who believed in our proposed changes, began successfully convincing the Early Majority. This was a crucial time in our transition to a faith-forming community in the postmodern era.

But we were not without casualties, and no church that ever seriously torques its way of living ever goes unscathed. As I read, studied, and prayed my way through guiding change in the congregations that I have served, one of the effects that I have come across is that as many as 20 percent of the people who were there when I arrived would not want to go through the kind of change necessary in order for the congregation to flourish. When I arrived at Christ Church, the attendance was approximately one hundred fifty, so—going in—I knew that about thirty people whom I would come to know and love as their pastor and brother in Christ would, for one reason or another, choose not to be participants in the preferred future that we were casting as our vision.

A statistic can seem impersonal and distant, but I can put names and faces with that 20 percent. As those at Christ Church began to commit themselves to our new way of organizing the church and others decided the change would be more than they could handle, I experienced sorrow when people I loved and appreciated said good-bye and left for other congregations.

One particular instance comes to mind. Much to my surprise (and joy), I showed up on my first Sunday at Christ Church to find that an old friend, a pastor's son himself, was a member. He was now married with two children and he and his wife were very active in the congregation. As we began to cast vision and implement changes, I thought he would enthusiastically support what we were trying to do to reach people for Jesus. I still remember the day when he came to the office and told me that, while he believed our direction was right and what we were doing was appropriate, it simply wasn't for him. He informed me that he and his family would be leaving the congregation and searching for another church. It was a very difficult moment and one that gave me great pause. I checked my intentions, my motivation, my prayer life, and the conviction I had that God was calling us to go in this particular direction. In the end, I blessed that family and several others, young and old, as they decided that the direction we were going as a congregation was not where they wanted to go.

In contrast to those moments of grief, I take solace from the fact that while those thirty to thirty-five persons chose to worship in other congregations, there were more than three hundred fifty people who came to Jesus by profession of faith and joined the life of Christ Church in the next five years. While we lost 20–25 percent of the worshiping congregation in the early stages of change, our congregation actually doubled as we pursued a more biblical way of doing church. The people who left Christ Church are still part of the Kingdom; they are actively involved in the congregations they attend, and I bless them for that, but I'm also thankful for the many more people who came to saving faith in Jesus Christ, grew in discipleship, and were trained for ministry.

Guided by these theological and practical convictions, we launched the largest campaign for change I had ever led. In the next chapter, I will lay out the kinds of changes we made, how they were implemented, and the congregational response to them. In the final chapter, I will add what I learned personally as well as what we learned as a congregation.

CHAPTER   FOUR

IMPLEMENTING CHANGE

I've been to a place where pastors have lost their jobs, a place where the abuse and pain have been so severe that pastors have found themselves in professional psychiatric care. In this place, pastors have lost their marriages, sacrificed the health of their children, and even at times nearly lost their faith. In this place the persecution of spiritual leadership is so intense that the survival of the leader, in and of itself, is a miracle. This place is not some foreign land; it is not under the oppression or rule of another nation. This most dangerous place is where a leader is seeking to transition a congregation from institution to movement.
—Erwin Raphael McManus, *An Unstoppable Force*

Keep in mind that everything you loathe about your current environment or organization was originally somebody's good idea.
—Andy Stanley, *The Next Generation Leader*

Changing any church's structure from a top-down, organizational, hierarchical, permission-withholding, pastor-centered, corporate model of the 1950s to a bottom-up, organic, collegial, permission-giving, team-oriented model centered around the spiritual giftedness of its members in the twenty-first century is a gargantuan task—especially in a denominational structure where processes and polity are decided upon apart from a church's given context. In fact, transitioning Christ United Methodist Church was one of the most difficult tasks of my ministry. However, difficult ministry tasks

49

often energize church renewal efforts and end up being more rewarding than simply improving the status quo. Remember the tree that had to be "ringed" in the introduction; a sacrifice had to be made, but it was minimal when compared to the harvest that would result.

In this chapter, I will lay out three ministry tools that will be helpful (if not essential) in a church's restructuring process. If your church has come to a place where change is non-negotiable for relevance in the twenty-first century, then I would encourage you to consider implementing the strategies discussed here. They were tools the Spirit was pleased to use at Christ Church, and they can work for you. *Caveat emptor*: no congregation is the same so you will have to make the necessary changes to fit your particular context.

Church Structure Task Force

At Christ Church, one of the first changes we made was to develop a Church Structure Task Force. The purpose of this team was to recommend a strategy that would better emulate the Spirit-led Apostolic age as well as strengthen the church's approach to community ministry. We asked mature, biblically informed members to serve on the committee, and charged them with analyzing our current structure and measuring it against the doctrine of spiritual gifts. This was a lengthy process but, like ringing a tree, change cannot be hurried.

Specifically, the Church Structure Task Force recommended the following changes:

- Dissolve and streamline the majority of the boards and committees under the church's former structure.
- Place existing ministries under the leadership of semi-autonomous ministry teams. These teams would take over the regular management and operation of those ministries.

The idea was that these ministry teams would recruit people with the desire, passion, and ownership necessary to see each ministry flourish. These recommendations were designed to intentionally move from filling positions by "slotting" to emphasizing the implementation of spiritual gifts in ministry.

According to the recommendations, each ministry team was to be led by a person with a passion for that particular ministry. With passion comes a sense of ownership, as well as a commitment to persevere. Harvard Business School professor Joseph Badaracco Jr. writes:

> Before beginning the difficult effort to change the world, even in a small way, men and women must assess how much they care. Often, the critical question is not about right and wrong. Put differently, moral concern is necessary but far from sufficient. The critical question is whether someone takes a problem personally enough to act, persist, endure, and soldier on (*Leading Quietly: An Unorthodox Guide to Doing the Right Thing* [Boston: Harvard Business School Press, 2002], 41).

For us, ownership fanned the desire to see individual ministries flourish. No longer were people gathering in monthly committee meetings to discuss the possibility of doing ministry sometime, someday. These ministry teams began to organize themselves around their ministry's mission and primary task. When they gathered together it was to minister, to act, to *do*.

When the ministry teams began to function out of this paradigm, we began to see exciting and innovative ministry developments. These teams were filled with the right people, serving in the right places, for the right reasons (Bruce Bugbee, Don Cousins, and Bill Hybels, *Network: The Right People . . . In the Right Places . . . For the Right Reasons* [Grand Rapids: Zondervan, 1994]). Out of their passion, they recruited others with similar passions to serve with them. They cast vision and called for commitment. They were contagious communities of people who really cared for and loved one another. Since most of the team members loved one another as much as they loved the ministry, there was a low turnover rate.

We required new ministry teams to follow a brief process for starting a new ministry that we outlined in our Mission Statement and Core Beliefs brochure. Among these Core Beliefs was the insistence that a sense of community, effective leadership, and an understanding of what it means to be gifted were essential ingredients for cultivating dynamic ministry teams. Once team members were on board with these convictions, we were able to give them permission to take risks and even fail. Why? Because they knew that the primary boundaries didn't have to do with seeking permission, but with loving, leading, and serving.

One area of unexpected difficulty in implementing our plan came from a key segment of the church leadership. Even though we had done as much as possible to develop a shared vision for restructuring the church, we had several key leaders who—midstream—decided they could no longer be supportive of the church's leadership and ministry. What made this more difficult is that several of these people had originally been key supporters and spokespersons for the restructuring effort. One of them was even a co-signer of the Church Structure Task Force Report. Eventually, they left our fellowship in search of a more traditional church structure. Their departure from the life of the church was very painful, and it complicated the transition. But we went on without them, and the church is much stronger today because of the systemic changes we initiated then.

The Church Structure Task Force served as a vanguard for our overall change effort. They helped us to make intelligent changes rather than knee-jerk reactions.

"Gifted to Serve" Implementation

One of the key elements in our restructuring process was the selection and implementation of a spiritual gift discovery system. After careful research into the nature of spiritual gifts, examining several spiritual gift discovery tools, and prayerful dialogue, the leadership team at Christ Church reached a consensus that we would implement a curriculum called *Network* (developed by Willow Creek in 1994, revised and re-released in 2004). It presently has the most holistic approach of any of the tools on the marketplace today.

We intended for *Network* to be more than a program. Our hope was that it would facilitate a whole new way of doing church because *Network* is designed to help people discover where God has planned for them to serve in ministry. The discovery and use of one's *passions* (where they should serve), *gifts* (how they can best serve), and *personal style* (how they should do what they are doing) helped members at Christ Church realize, many for the first time, that ministry and fulfillment can—and should—intersect in a believer's life. We quickly made this an enduring value in our congregational life. We purchased the *Network* curriculum and began to implement it into the life and ministry of our church, revamping it with a bit of Wesleyan flavor and renaming it "Gifted to Serve."

There were two phases in the implementation process of *Network*. Phase One involved the formation of a *Network* team, preparation of a proposal, presentation of the proposal to the senior leadership of the congregation, and finally having the senior leadership personally experience *Network Implementation Guide* (1994, 16–22). That's right: there was no point in promoting a new way to be the church if we senior leaders weren't going to go through it ourselves. We filled out a workbook and attended sessions just like everyone else would.

Once Phase One was completed and all of the senior leaders had personally interacted with the material and its challenges, we were set to involve the whole church. Acting on the core belief that "God has equipped every Christian with skills, gifts and passions to be used in the mission and ministry of the church throughout the world," we began the process of introducing *Network* as the tool we would use to develop this belief into a lasting value at Christ Church. This brought us to Phase Two.

In Phase Two, we integrated our existing ministry leaders into the *Network* process. In other words, we took what our leaders were already doing and looked at how our existing ministries would influence our presentation of *Network* and how *Network* would impact our existing ministries. Once this process was complete, we were in a position to develop ministry position (job) descriptions to place people more accurately where they were best "Gifted to Serve" (*Network Implementation Guide*, 1994, 26–29).

One unanticipated challenge was the length of time needed to develop accurate job descriptions for ministry positions throughout Christ Church's life and ministry. When you think of how many different areas of responsibility there are in a mid-to-large sized church, this should not be all that surprising. *The good news is that writing such job descriptions is work that seldom has to be done twice.* Positions may expand and change, but the arduous task of writing each description from the ground up should only happen once. An added bonus to this tedious work is that writing job descriptions helps a church become quite clear on what is expected of a volunteer. Many Christians become lukewarm in their service, not because they don't like the work, but because they are thrown into a ministry position and subsequently ignored. Nobody likes to work without clear objectives and goals. Taking the time to provide concise-but-clear job descriptions will boost the confidence levels of those who serve.

The Buzz

Overall, the "Gifted to Serve" ministry was a positive experience. Rather than slotting people into positions that didn't fit them, the "Gifted to Serve" program helped people discover where they were gifted and set them free to do the work of the ministry. Some people discovered they were not serving where they were gifted, and we encouraged them to get involved in other places of ministry. This created some temporary holes in our leadership, but we believed that God would raise up the right leadership with the passions, gifts, and personal style necessary to fill those holes. Most of the time, that is exactly what happened. When that didn't happen, it was often the case that the given ministry needed to die anyway.

The overwhelming majority of respondents stated that "Gifted to Serve" met and *exceeded their expectations*. People understood the purpose of the program and were able to articulate it. We were cultivating an Ephesians 4 ethos in our church, and it wasn't just the leadership—it was what Bill Hybels calls "the power of every-body" (*The Volunteer Revolution: Unleashing the Power of Everybody* [Grand Rapids: Zondervan, 2004].

Participants also expressed a strong belief in the accuracy of the course's ability to help participants discover their passions, gifts, and style. Follow-up conversations revealed that the combination of passions, gifts, and style helped people further clarify their unique, God-given niche for ministry within the church. Especially helpful was the information regarding how social style bears on the way God has distinctly wired us for ministry. These were areas that had been ignored or undervalued in the nominating process.

Finally able to understand their place in ministry, "Gifted to Serve" participants could weed out extraneous activities that had previously drained them of energy and excitement for ministry. They were now able to focus themselves on the ministry to which they had been called and for which they were gifted. In addition, participants came to understand they were *ministering in response to grace* . . . not out of a sense of duty to the church. This responsiveness to grace was a newfound source of joy for many members in our church, mainly because they could finally differentiate between serving the church and being obedient to Christ. They were in ministry because they realized that God had gifted and called them by the grace of Jesus Christ, not because the church had needs.

As members proceeded through the "Gifted to Serve" program, enthusiasm—visible and palpable—grew. People began talking to others about the program and its fruit.

"Gifted to Serve" Areas of Struggle

After the implementation of the "Gifted to Serve" program, I became aware of several areas that would have to be tweaked in order to achieve the maximum impact we believed the program could offer. Let me forecast some of the issues you might face in implementing this strategy.

First, your people are *busy*, and they view service as one time commitment among many. We had several people who completed "Gifted to Serve," but did not use the information in order to link up with a ministry. Their default excuse was that they didn't have enough time. Of course, most people have the time to do what they perceive to be important. The challenge for the church is to create ministry opportunities that are compelling enough for a person to place above other possible ways to spend time. People who are fulfilled in ministry see what they do as having an eternal significance in the lives of other people. Therefore, they are willing to rearrange their schedules to include ministry if it is going to have an impact in the lives of real people.

Second, we sometimes struggled to help people identify their *passion* for ministry. Further conversation revealed that the reason for this is that most of us are not used to thinking about work and service in terms of passion. Our culture tends to tell us what we are going to do, when we are going to do it, and how it will be done. The former organizational structure of our congregation had fostered this tendency. It took time to get people to dream big dreams about ministry, and to recognize that those dreams might be the initial expressions of God-given passion. However, after people began to get a feel for their passion for ministry, we were able to launch dynamic ministries (i.e., Parish Nurse, *Serv'em* [servant evangelism], and Christ House [an effort to provide transitional housing for the homeless in our community]).

Third, discovering one's gifts, passion, and style is only the first step. Significant attention must be placed on the *consultation process* as well as *training* for those who step forward in ministry.

Ideally, these steps are easier to take if you have a director of lay ministries (possibly a ministry team in its own right) who supervises the consultation process with great sensitivity. You may even offer to send a few passionate members for specialized training through conferences and workshops.

Fourth, it is important to understand that some people are hesitant to become involved in ministry for the following reasons:

- They don't see themselves as a "leaders," and they assume that "serving" in the church means becoming a leader.
- They are afraid that once they get into a place of service, they are stuck there for life. Several shared that they were hesitant to make that kind of commitment because they feared being in the wrong niche, and didn't want to spend their time doing something they don't enjoy.
- Our congregation did not have enough ministries to people outside the walls of the church who lived in our community. One of the learnings of the "Gifted to Serve" course was that we had several people in our congregation with a heart for the poor, homeless, and disenfranchised in our community. This was a pressing need since Erie, Pennsylvania had a high percentage of homeless children and ethnic minority children under the poverty limit. Once we gave our people the permission to dream about their God-given passion, they began to develop a variety of ministries designed to alleviate human suffering and reach our community. The Parish Nurse Ministry, Serv'em, and the Christ House Ministry Team are all examples of ministries that are in existence today that never would have been if people had not been encouraged to reach beyond the walls of our church.

Fifth, although we tried to be proactive and clear on the nature of spiritual gifting, there tended to be confusion about the difference between *spiritual gifts* and *natural talents*. I suggest that you go to great lengths to differentiate the key differences thoroughly in your written and spoken promotions.

Finally, in addition to struggling with creating the many needed job descriptions, we also suffered from a lack of implementation consultants. Ideally, each individual proceeding through "Gifted to Serve" would meet one-on-one with an advisor or consultant, who would suggest appropriate places to serve based on their course results. We just didn't have enough people to invest that kind of time. If at all possible, take proactive steps to make this a priority. It does the community of faith no good if we train individuals for ministry and then fail to help them find their distinct niche for service. By the second or third time through, we made it our goal to not only have a book of all the ministry position descriptions at Christ Church but to also have trained consultants who would help to match people with the positions in that book.

"Gifted to Serve" Summary

Over time, "Gifted to Serve" became a living core value of our church. At the opening session of "Gifted to Serve," each person was asked why he or she was taking the training. One of the participants said, "It has become obvious to me that this is not just a program. Our leadership has bought into "Gifted to Serve." This is a core value of our church. I want to be involved where I can make the most difference in Jesus' name!" People began to recognize this was not just another program, but something we were intentionally weaving into the very DNA of our church.

"Gifted to Serve" became a highly recognizable course in the life of Christ Church. Offer something like it three to four times per year and around the time new members are received into your church family. This will enable you and them to understand their areas of gifting, passion, and style and should initiate their involvement in ministry. By doing this, the program actually doubles as an assimilation tool.

"Gifted to Serve" also helped us discover the need to celebrate new ministries and gracefully allow obsolete ministries to pass away if there wasn't anyone gifted and called to serve in those capacities. For example, we had difficulty finding leadership for the traditional United Methodist Women for four years. Finally, someone asked the question the rest of us were afraid to ask: "Does God want us to have this ministry? And if God does, then why can't we find leadership?" After prayerful discussion, we celebrated the forty years of ministry contributed by the United Methodist Women and allowed them to disband. However, we did not give up on women's ministries; we continued to support those ministries for which God raised up leadership. One year, we sent a busload of women to the "Bring Back the Joy" Conference in Buffalo, New York. Out of that conference grew a vital ministry, which the former United Methodist Women would most likely never have developed. Remember the ringed tree.

Likewise, we celebrated new ministries whenever we could. We shared their successes with the congregation through announcements and parish papers. We nurtured fledgling ministries with encouragement and resources. We tried to make sure everyone involved in a new ministry knew we were committed to success. We did whatever we could to dispel any notion that they were "doing time," but instead encouraged them to see lifelong service as a normative part of life in the body of Christ.

"Gifted to Serve" was a great tool that helped us refocus. The congregation began to see ministry as something they were gifted to do and as something that was done in service to God in response to grace. Again, not everything about this process was easy, but it was worth it! I don't know of anything more fulfilling as a minister of the gospel than to see God's ministers (all the children of God) discover what they were put on earth to do.

Training for Leadership and Community (TLC)

In the months that followed the initial changes, communication and supervision of ministry teams began to be carried out as per the design and recommendations of the Church Structure Task Force Report. However, we began to discover inconsistencies between our original plan and its implementation. Some of our leadership teams overseeing the ministry teams were not providing the level of communication, training, and accountability the ministry teams needed. They quickly became in danger of functioning like the old, bureaucratic committees. We also lacked a genuine sense of community and cooperation between the teams, as well as a clearly defined training process for our ministry team leaders.

As a result, we began a monthly leadership training and community-building ministry. It was called TLC, which stands for Training for Leadership and Community. The church staff coordinated it; leaders of our ministry teams, small group leaders, and Sunday school teachers were invited to attend. The steps we took at TLC were intended to help each ministry team become a disciple-making community, as well as provide the leadership training and community development that a church needs to be effective.

The purpose of TLC was to provide an arena where leaders of the church's ministry teams, small groups, and Sunday school classes could come together to celebrate our shared life, be trained for leadership within our church, communicate about ministry and pressing issues, and develop a sense of accountability to the mission statement and core beliefs of the church.

TLC Evaluation

Leadership and community development are going to be crucial to any church seeking to change from a power-hoarding entity to a power-giving ministry. In fact, without careful attention given to these two important areas, it is my belief that change simply will not happen. The jump can be made—as is evidenced by Christ Church's story—but people will only jump if we as ministers show them and train them (remember Eph. 4:12).

In modernity, the pastor held all the power and made all the decisions. We wanted to implement a more biblical approach that would disperse decision-making power within the church family. As the leadership trained others for leadership and service, we were providing a more harmonious balance of power. Frankly, we were leading better.

In our attempt to develop Training for Leadership and Community (TLC), we made some great strides toward achieving this kind of balance. This is not to say that it was flawless; we certainly had our fair share of "learning opportunities" (a.k.a. frustrating pains in the neck). In the end though, TLC brought us closer to having a bottom-up, organic, collegial, permission-giving, team-oriented model centered on the spiritual giftedness of its members in the twenty-first century. Those who became involved in TLC understood its purpose, valued its components, and felt it should be required of all leaders. Even those who did not participate in the initial TLC program recognized the value of and need for training, communication, and the sharing of ideas. They, too, had experienced the sense of isolation that was commonplace among ministry leaders in our new system, and saw the value of attempting to rectify this problem.

In the end, TLC was a very valuable program. It served its purpose of training and equipping leaders in our church and developing community through worship and communion.

TLC Areas of Struggle

Even though participants understood the purpose of TLC, we quickly learned that many came to the training sessions with very high, and perhaps impossible, expectations. Because servants in our church had rarely been brought together for the purpose of building community, we started slow. In fact, we spent little time on leadership training because we wanted people to know and be known. As a result, participants evaluated the community building aspect of TLC as being very strong, and the leadership-training portion as very weak. Share up front what your participants should expect to gain from the program.

Second, make accountability and communication a high priority, even in a permission-giving organization. The participants pointed out that accountability and information sharing was lacking among our ministry leaders. Further conversation revealed that several folks, while enjoying the new permission-giving style, felt as if they were all alone in ministry. Sometimes, in the thrill of executing change, leaders tend to push the baby birds out of the nest without really knowing whether or not they can fly. We learned that one the hard way.

Third, make TLC (or a program like it) a requirement for all church leaders. Initially, we had a low percentage of participation by ministry team leaders, small group leaders, and Sunday school teachers. Part of it was that people claimed to be too busy, and part of it was that anything new takes awhile to catch on. But as people experienced the benefits of TLC, they became convinced that participation in TLC was essential for effective leadership and should be required of anyone desiring to lead.

Fourth, one practical suggestion is to start and end on time. As leaders, we can gain a great deal of trust with our constituents if we show them that we value their time. When we do what we say we are going to do on the little things, people tend to trust that we will do the same on the big things. Believe it or not, your credibility is on the line every minute you run over the stated ending time.

Fifth, people in North America are simply too busy! Blame consumerism, materialism, or whatever "ism" you want, but the ministry of the church often fails to dent the priority system of many of our church leaders. But if the church offers a compelling cause, people will be willing to rearrange their priorities to include that cause. So what do we need to do? Offer a compelling cause! Vision causes the heart to beat faster, and casting vision is the responsibility of the leader. If you cast a pulse-quickening vision, people will respond. If you are not gifted in compelling people to get involved, then recruit and empower someone who is!

Finally, select acronyms wisely. Sometimes the simplicity of a recognizable and popular acronym can send people in the wrong direction. There was a general lack of understanding about TLC's purpose among a large majority of members who did not participate in the initial TLC session. The acronym, TLC, is catchy, but the outsider does not know what it means. We decided after the first TLC class that we would include the words "Training for Leadership and Community" in every correspondence about TLC so that even those who decided not to participate would get a feel for the direction in which we were heading.

TLC Summary

TLC was a great way to develop the kind of community, communication, training, and accountability necessary for facilitating the life and ministry of the church. We understood some would balk at making this a requirement, but having seen the isolation that easily develops without such a structure in place, we felt justified in our stance that participation be mandatory.

To ensure everyone knew this was expected, we scheduled face-to-face conversations with those who served in leadership, but who had—for various reasons—not consistently attended TLC sessions. Sadly, some chose to no longer provide leadership in our church because of this requirement, but we believed the benefit of TLC for the total life and health of the church outweighed their departure.

Second, rather than meeting on a weekly basis, we recommended that TLC be scaled back to every other week. It is an odd custom that committees must meet every week. I hate to be the one to shock you with this, but you don't always have to meet once a week for everything. It may be a very freeing experience for you to try the biweekly method with some of your meetings. In our biweekly TLC meeting we would:

- Start the gathering with singing and praise.
- Continue the practice of meeting in small groups at round tables. This helps to foster fellowship and builds relationships.
- Dedicate time for sharing where we saw God at work in our community over the previous month.
- Choose one topic for discussion and training. This allowed us to go into greater detail while covering less material.
- Allow time for discussion and practical application. Leaders were able to take the principles back to their ministry team and apply them there.
- Cast vision and establish goals together.
- Close with worship and communion.
- Complete a TLC feedback form, and implement suggestions where applicable.

Finally, we decided to use the first Monday of the month on off-TLC weeks for ministry teams to gather at the church for community building and planning. This was an avenue we used to showcase others who were using their various gifts, passions, and styles for ministry in response to God's grace. Again, their ministry was not as much in service to the church as it was worship unto God.

A Renewed Body

Around New Year's Day, it is impossible to miss the avalanche of diet ads, commercials, and promotions aimed at individuals making resolutions for the new year. Most promise mind-blowing results guaranteed to happen virtually overnight. "By taking this pill (or using this plan, or buying this home gym) you can have a new body!"

At Christ Church, we didn't have a vision for a new body. We also knew our desired changes wouldn't happen overnight. But we methodically pressed on, trusting the Spirit to empower us and transform us into a renewed body—one with a sense of purpose and vitality. The Church Structure Task Force, "Gifted to Serve," and TLC were vital components of our transition. These ideas can be adapted for use in most church contexts and can help faithful Christians find their place of service so that the whole body works as it should.

TRANSFERABLE LESSONS

I n closing, let me share a few life learnings that emerged from the Church Structure Task Force, "Gifted to Serve," and TLC:

Expect the unexpected.

When we think about restructuring a church, it doesn't seem all that complicated: you move a few boxes around, you change a few titles, and you make sure the people serving are fit for the job. But even something as unspectacular as church structure invites political maneuvering. No matter how small your church is, if you're going to attempt something like this kind of task force, don't expect it to come off without a snag.

Warm bodies don't produce sizzling results.

Churches are perhaps the only organizations that select people to perform crucial tasks on the basis of their willingness alone. How would a Fortune 500 company or a professional sports team look if they added workers and players simply because they had a positive attitude and wanted to do a good job? Why is it that "any warm body" is good enough for God? Tim Stevens writes, "Many times churches place too much emphasis on *availability* and not enough emphasis on *ability*" (Stevens and Morgan, *Simply Strategic Stuff* [Loveland: Group, 2004], 77). There is nothing wrong with aiming high when you're looking to select someone for kingdom work (see Romans 12:6-8).

Make "being known" a requirement.

In some ways, this counsel comes from many churches' tendency to fill slots with warm bodies. One of the questions the leadership has to ask is, "Do we *know* these people?" It is risky to put people in positions of responsibility without knowing them well. Churches should not put new members (or nonmembers) in ministry positions for at least six months after becoming a part of the church body. People have to know and be known in order to minister from a family perspective instead of one that sees ministry as "something good church people do."

Repeatedly emphasize to your congregation that change requires sacrifice.

Do your best to make it nearly impossible for anyone to complain that they weren't warned. When we began to shift from a top-down, bureaucratic institution to a bottom-up, dynamic body, how we utilized our facilities caused some discomfort among members. Simply said, space could no longer be "owned" by a particular group. The older adult Sunday school classes, which had the largest rooms, often had the smallest attendances. We changed the room assignments (and upset a few people) in order to optimize use of our facilities. Further, the kitchen was no longer the "holy of holies" to which only a privileged few had access; we opened it up to small groups who wanted to have meals together. From the choir room to the chapel, we placed a moratorium on all claims to private ownership of church space among groups. The sacrifice involved actually increased buy-in among members as they saw we were serious about making changes.

Budget to match your priorities and values.

We began to challenge our people to develop a "Jerusalem, Judea, Samaria, to the ends of the earth" mission effort, but in order for it to materialize, we needed to grow our mission budget. It's one thing to make a grand pronouncement during a sermon that "we're serious about missions," but unless your budget reflects tangible giving efforts to mission-related activities and agencies, you're allowing your people to believe missions happen by themselves. Missions require money. Build your highest priorities and values into the budget; otherwise, you can probably expect them to be swept under the rug of immediate concerns.

Develop alternative worship celebrations and times to meet different populations who are functionally unchurched.

Not everyone wants to worship at 9:00 A.M. on Sunday morning to organ music while wearing formal attire. Utilize different worship styles and methods. If you need to, arrange for different people on your staff to preach. Honor creativity and diversity.

Be prepared for over-correction and under-participation.

We sometimes experienced problems between leaders and team members in the "Gifted to Serve" process. At one end, the leaders didn't always catch the vision. Some participants threw themselves into ministry ideas that grew bigger and faster than we ever dreamed and the leaders found themselves fighting the temptation to "rein it in." At the other end, some members didn't quite grasp the intention of the program. It took time and patience to make the transition, from committees that gathered to talk rather than do, to a ministry of teams centered on meeting a real need through gifted members of the congregation and community. Even so, some of our "team leaders" continued to function like committees and nothing new happened.

Require new ministry leaders to formulate a S.M.A.R.T. plan.

S.M.A.R.T. plans are Simple and Strategic...Measurable ...Attainable only through faith...Rational...and Timelined. Rather than simply devising goals, **S.M.A.R.T.** plans chart the journey in ways that won't overwhelm the new leader.

Interview potential ministry leaders thoroughly.
We had a clear set of questions to ask persons who were feeling called to a form of ministry: Have you prayed about this? Does it fit within the heart of our mission and values? Are you willing to recruit a ministry team to work with you? Do you have a **S.M.A.R.T.** plan? What do you need from the leadership to succeed? Look for more than a rich and diverse history of ministry experience or charisma; make sure the person has the character necessary to follow through and endure setbacks joyfully.

Put in ministry only those people who are willing to be trained and consulted.
Many members who had been a part of the church for a long time were resistant to making this change. "Why do I need to come to TLC if I'm in charge of painting the classrooms?" Their perspective came from an assumption that the church that got us to where we were was the same church that was going to reach our community. In contrast, we found that newer Christians as well as newer members of our fellowship were more likely to commit to training and consultation because we emphasized it up front when they first came to us. The early adopters were easy to convince, but it took a long time to gain the approval of the early majority. In fact, I moved to a new ministry setting before this aspect of our life together was firmly in place.

Prepare to, at times, run redundant systems.
We found that, as hard as we tried, there were a few entities within our congregation that could not shift from one style to another. In order to keep some folks engaged, and because we could not let certain administrative groups simply disappear, a handful of entities (the standing committees of Finance and Trustees to name two) continued to function in their former ways.

You cannot over-communicate.
Transitioning from a top-down, organizational, hierarchical, permission-withholding, pastor-centered, corporate model of the

1950s ministry style to a bottom-up, organic, collegial, permission-giving, team-oriented model centered around the spiritual gifted-ness of its members in the twenty-first century will result in a dismantling of previous communication systems throughout the church. This will cause unease among members who were used to giving and receiving information a certain way. For us, the former way of doing ministry might not have been the most efficient or effective, but the people who had invested in it certainly knew what was going on. A new system that gutted those avenues of communication, and the initial months of team-oriented ministry, revealed that the right hand didn't know what the left hand was doing. There was much confusion, and a "go back to Egypt" committee began to express itself. Truthfully, we had only ourselves to blame; we had not done a good job anticipating communication needs or leadership development among the team leaders. As mentioned previously, TLC was developed to address those needs.

Don't let growth be an option.

Not everyone will want your congregation to grow. "Do we want to grow?" is not the right question. To say "no" is to stand against everything that the church is supposed to stand for. The real question is "are we willing to pay the price of growing?" That question is not as easy to answer, and will test the soul and strength of the leadership of any congregation.

Structure is not an end in itself.

The real power behind congregational growth is whether people who come to the church can become a part of the life-changing, world-altering movement of God in the redemption of creation. People want to be a part of something that is dramatically bigger than they are.

Teach thoroughly on the Holy Spirit and spiritual gifts.

Some of your people have probably been burned by overzealous charismatics and will be scared to death of the Holy Spirit and the spiritual gifts. The wise leader will take the necessary amount of time to explore and teach soundly in this area.

Disagree agreeably.

Have "hospitality of soul"—make room for questions, expression of dissonance, and push-back. People need to know you are not trying to pull a fast one on them, but are really working out of a solid biblical, theological foundation that, at its heart, is good for the church.

Remember that the "Nominating Committee" practice of slotting people is more efficient, but not more effective.

To be sure, spending months in vision casting, structure changing, and ministry aligning is more complex on the front end than the work of the Nominating Committee. But in the end, it offers a much better chance of leading people into long-term service because through it people will function where God has called and gifted them to serve.

Cultivate a "draw" to TLC.

All your training opportunities need to be done with high quality. If people trust that the proper amount of preparation, thought, and creativity has been put into your training events, they will come. But if they sense that your version of TLC is repeatedly thrown together at the last minute because it's not high on your priority list, guess what? They'll push it down on their priority list, too.

In spite of the time commitment involved, don't be afraid to approach your leaders and ask them to meet for prayer.

It is always a good idea to get the ministry team leaders together for vision building and prayer. Not only will it increase ownership among your leaders, it will prevent other members from thinking this is all "your" doing. Seek and hear from the Lord together in order to receive power and insight as a team.